A Paignton
SCRAPBOOK

PEGGY PARNELL

The
History
Press

First published in 2007 by Sutton Publishing

Reprinted in 2013 by
The History Press
The Mill, Brimscombe Port,
Stroud, Gloucestershire, GL5 2QG
www.thehistorypres.co.uk

British Library Cataloguing in Publication Data
A catalogue record for this book is available from the British Library.

ISBN 978-0-7509-4739-8

Dedication

*To Eileen, with many thanks for her enduring help and advice,
to David, my husband, for his constant supply of meals and
never-ending support
and to my life-long friend Pat.*

Typeset in 11/12.5pt Ehrhardt.
Typesetting and origination by
Sutton Publishing.
Printed and bound in Great Britain by
Marston Book Services Limited, Didcot

Contents

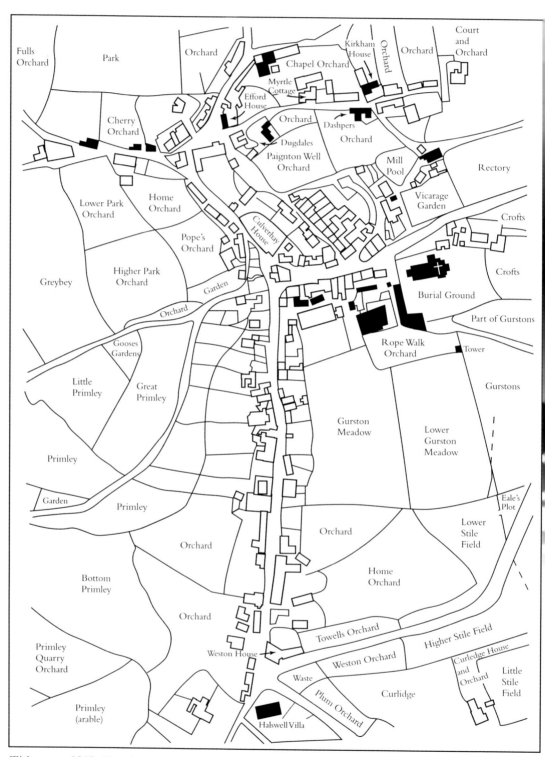

Tithe map, 1840. (*Based on a map from Devon Record Office*)

Introduction

Old Devonians were once renowned for their romancing when relating local stories; you could say it was a form of journalese, perhaps brought about by their isolation here in the remote south west of England. However, this collection of tales has developed into a pudding full of surprises spanning different periods of life with different stories about different people associated with one of Devon's ancient 'burg' towns (an enclosed gated area), called Paignton. The majority of yarns are from between the early nineteenth century to the mid-twentieth century and are spun not only by those who are born and bred Paigntonians, but also Paigntonians by adoption!

Some stories are far older, showing just how much Paignton was allied through farming and historical events with nearby towns including Brixham, Totnes and Newton Abbot. Then there are those 'old un's' long since gone, who used to spin yarns that became legendary in their time, coloured and heightened further by later generations in the warmth of a local pub, helped no doubt by numerous glasses of cider. OK, so one or two of the yarns may have been told over and over, with tongue in cheek, while others are of human and historical merit, but all are based in fact no matter how old or by whom told and how much they may have changed in their storytelling.

Please accept my apologies for any inaccuracies, for as explained, many of the accounts are as they have been described or written by others. Now dig deep and enjoy discovering the many and various yarns, large and small, old and recent as related by numerous Paigntonians with some additional tit-bits just for the fun of it.

Peggy Parnell
Paignton, 2007

The author has made every effort to contact the various sources she used in compiling this book and apologises to anyone who may not have received notification of her intent.

Taking into consideration the difficulties of covering so many stories and varying activities in Paignton and its surrounding area, the author also apologises for any mis-quotations or errors that may have inadvertently been made and the omittance of several stories, which was beyond her control.

Acknowledgements

With thanks to the following people for their contributions:
Michael Adams; Roy & Tina Authors; Estelle & Adrian Barnard; Dave Blackmore; Mary Bridgeman; Ernest Britton; Brixham Museum; Buckfastleigh Station; Diane Caine; Wendy Caplan; Brian Carter; Pat Chubb; Cyril Clark; Gail Collins, Primley Home; W.G. Couldrey; Bill Coysh; Arthur Day; Devon Record Office; Devonshire Association; Michael Dowdell; English Heritage; Dr Epstein; Jill Farrant; Betty Fuller; Derek Gore; Alistair Grant; David Head; Donald Head; Leo Head; Leslie Head; *Herald & Express*; Kevin Hodgkinson; M. Holman; George Hunter; Peggy Jackman; Margaret Jeffries; Moyra Jenkins; Sharon Knight, Collaton Fishacre; Bob LeMarchant; John Mann; Ingrid Marsh; Mrs G. Masters; Revd Gillian Maude; T. Moss; Paignton Library; Paignton Preservation & Local History Society; David Parnell; Eric Parnell; Sam Partridge; Frank Pearce; John Perrett; Margaret Plummer; Janette Procter; E. Purton; D. Ricks; John Risdon; Nigel Rossiter; Ken Rowe; Marion Smith; Ann Stockwell, Hill House; Mike Thompson; Sheila Thorndyke; Torbay Council; Torbay Council Estates Office; Torquay Museum; Torquay Reference Library; Revd Tubbs; Mary Tully; Brian & Joan Vickery; David Walden; A. Ward; Jill Webber, Torbay School of Dancing; Mary & Ron Wellens; Mike Wells; Yvonne Wells; Geraldine Wheatley; Pat Wilby; Susan Woodward; Ted Woolvet; John Wright.

CHAPTER ONE

Some Early Stories

A NAME IS A NAME!

Over time there have been at least thirty different ways of spelling Paignton since the Normans gave their French version of the name to the town in 1066, so it isn't surprising to discover that on completion of the railway in 1859 there was some controversy about how the name should be spelt, particularly on destination boards.

Some time before the opening of the railway, Brunel's surveyor arrived in town to begin listing the names of towns and villages along the track line into Paignton. Somewhat confused by the local variations in spelling the town name, he was advised to consult the Steward of the Manor and the vicar, which he did, but this led to even further confusion when these worthy men couldn't agree. The vicar assured Brunel's surveyor it was Paignton, while the steward, equally adamant, insisted it was Paington, so to satisfy them both the surveyor put on his report 'Paignton or Paington'. With the station completed, name boards were duly set up on each platform, one as 'Paignton' and the other as 'Paington'.

These two boards remained thus for many years, causing frequent criticism and much amusement, until the day a new stationmaster asked the postmaster which way the postal authorities spelt the name and was told it was 'Paignton'. The worthy stationmaster decided there and then that this must be the correct spelling so promptly had 'Paington' blotted out, much to the regret of Paigntonians who enjoyed teasing visitors with the conundrum. As it happens time and research have shown that the steward was probably right all along! (W.E. Couldrey, *Memories*, 1932)

OLD PN'TUN

Old Pn'tun, as the locals used to call their town, grew up around the lovely eleventh-century parish church with such descriptive street names as Mill Lane, Well Street, Duck Street (renamed Princes Street at the local residents' request in 1881), and Church Street, which in the eighteenth century became known as Culverhey, possibly relating to a dove/pigeon-house that existed in the mid-sixteenth-century, but may also refer to an old cross. The name Culverhey, however doesn't refer to the bishop's huge culverts that run under Church Street from the nearby Bishop's Palace, dating from around the same period as the church. Well Street originates from an ancient holy well that gushed out a strong flow of ice-cold water towards the sea, the power of which the bishops harnessed for turning their corn mill, although it is thought there may have been a Saxon mill before then. It has also been said the Romans knew the settlement as 'Mollendunam', meaning the place of the mill; although it is considered highly unlikely, there are reasons to think there might be some truth in this as some Roman coins were found in the St Michael's area, albeit some years ago now.

When the bishops moved into the manor they would have required considerable quantities of wine for their church ceremonies as well as for personal consumption. On the north-westerly side of the Bishop's Palace a hill ascends sharply allowing a sheltered south-easterly aspect, a good position for their vineyards, and thus Winner Street (ME *winyard* – Oxford English Dictionary) got its name, but this street didn't start to develop as a trading area until after Henry VIII closed down the Bishop's Palace and from then on the bishop's vineyards were neglected. From time unknown beneath this hillside were at least three court-farms (small enclosed units) all in the form of strip farms and all long since disappeared, although there is one building with an entrance arch and passageway through which can still be seen remnants of old buildings and steps leading up onto Winner Hill.

An eighteenth-century painting of Church Street, the site of the Charter Fair of 1294–5. (*Peggy Parnell*)

The earliest known drawing of Paignton's old mill, *c*. 1835. (*Peggy Parnell*, *PP&LHS*)

It is just possible one or two of these enclosed farms may have been associated with the bishops' vineyards that once existed on this hill, but over time became altered to suit the problems faced by the population that inevitably followed the bishops' departure. Certainly, by the late sixteenth century apple orchards for a growing cider industry became all important, so the arrangements of these farms were probably altered to accommodate the inevitable changes taking place, in particular the introduction of a new type of cabbage called flat-poles, used for cattle feed, as well as a sweet verity for culinary use. With the increase in corn production, corn-merchants and nurserymen appeared. By the nineteenth century these court farms had become family-run enterprises complete within themselves; with cottages, stables, milking parlours, or whatever, depending on the type of work being carried out within them. The best known was seventeenth-century Distin's Court, which by the late nineteenth century became so badly neglected it was finally demolished to allow the Baptist church to extend. By this time cattle slaughtering had expanded into a large industry, creating a considerable number of butchers' shops, and as the population expanded so did alehouses to cater for their alcohol needs.

Distins Court captured on film, before its demolition in the late nineteenth century. (*Eileen Donovan*)

WHEN BISHOPS HELD PAIGNTON

Markets existed in most medieval towns and were profitable to their owners. During the thirteenth and fourteenth centuries townspeople could apply for a charter to secure freedom from external control and gain various privileges, but the Bishops of Exeter held the old 'burg' – which meant that in 1295 it would have been Bishop Bitton who applied to the king for Paignton's charter. Because of this the town missed out on any municipal rights.

The medieval system was complicated, for if your town was unfortunate enough to be held, as Paignton was, by the church then it was the bishop who collected tolls and fees (stallagium – about 50p today) from the traders and occasionally from the customers, and sometimes even charged booth and stall holders the same. Even so, before any market could start trading permission had to be gained from the local judge (reeve) for the legal right to trade with outsiders from other towns across the area. In most cases the king ratified this, but in Paignton's case it's more likely to have been the bishop. Whether king or bishop, his glove would almost certainly have been sent as a sign of approval. Ceremonies such as this were commonplace and usually accompanied by a poem and very likely, as happened in many towns at the opening of their market, a shower of hot pennies that would be thrown down from a window onto a crowd of children below.

A COVERING OF STRAW

In the early 1900s, people were still using pony and trap and goods were delivered in horse-drawn vans. The roads and streets were not tarmac as they are today, not even sanded and sprayed, with the result that they soon became rutted and bumpy; consequently the iron-tyred horse-drawn vehicles crashed deafeningly through the streets making a terrible din. If someone was very ill, a thick covering of straw was laid on the road outside the sick person's house to abate the noise, which was done for several days outside Jack Preston's butcher's shop, while his wife lay dying in a room above.

FAIRS WERE DIFFERENT

Fairs were slightly different from markets, the latter being held for the convenience of the townspeople and those living close by, whereas fairs attracted visitors from far and wide and were nearly always associated with a saint or nearby shrine. In Paignton's case they were granted jointly in 1294–5 on the Vigil Feast and Morrow of Trinity Sunday. With the market and fair being as one they were held simultaneously in Church Street (Fore Street) in front of the 'Porch', which according to W.G. Couldrey probably meant the palace entrance.

In many towns and cities, as for example Exeter during its Lammas Fair, a large stuffed glove was paraded through the town and fixed to the Guildhall roof. In the case of an ancient 'burg' like Paignton the glove was probably fixed to a staging, most likely erected outside the west door of the parish church. This age-old custom not only denoted the opening of a fair, but also signalled to the outside merchants they could now enter the town without fear of arrest.

Paigntonians enjoying the Church Street fair in 1935. (*Paignton Observer*)

Interestingly, Paignton's stocks were always situated outside the church ready for any troublemaking that inevitably followed a day of cider-drinking!

In 1935, following the Silver Jubilee celebrations, the residents of Church Street turned back the centuries when they recreated the town's ancient market and fayre of 1295. Much merriment took place with dancing in the street, fancy costumes and, of course, the old stocks set ready for use! There were roasted chestnuts, sizzling sausages and fabulous ham sandwiches, the latter obtained from Billy Hooper's shop on the corner of Crown & Anchor Way (one of the town's many butchers and site of the seventeenth-century coaching inn), probably all washed down with pints of good local cider. Behind Hooper's shop was an old slaughter building. On this occasion it was used for anyone who wished to rid themselves of any inhibitions by throwing stones at a pile of old

The public gathers to hear the announcement of
the opening of the 1935 Church Street fair.
(*Paignton Observer*)

Church Street in about 1900. In the centre of the photograph is Martin's Drapery and Carter's sweet shop. To the right, out of sight, is Osborn, the tailor and to the left is Well Street. (*T. Moss*)

china. This fair certainly had a medieval air complete with a town crier, a well-known dairyman called Leo Head who, while shouting 'Oyez! Oyez!', rang his one and only ice-cream bell complete with crack!

The years passed and shops like Martin's drapery, Osborn's tailoring and Carter's sweet shop were demolished, and with them went the heart of old Church Street. Remembered in particular was a small Down's Syndrome girl who used to sit on the pavement outside Carter's, a large metal grating in front of her where many a customer lost their small change. This grill covered the bishop's diverted stream that once flowed down towards the corn mill. These old buildings (Martin's drapery and Carter's sweet shop) had character and were of a good age. As if this wasn't enough, in addition to their demise the island cottages at the top of Church Street were also removed – all sacrificed for road widening.

Even so, right up to the mid-1950s Church Street with its fine parish church was still to a great extent the hub of old Paignton, where during the summer months personalities like Miss Eggins would sit at the top of the Bishop's Tower selling 'objets d'art' in aid of the parish church.

Now, in the twenty-first century, most of Paignton's old buildings, subjected over the years to so many changes, have either been altered out of all recognition or completely demolished, but a few are still left.

CHAPTER TWO
Tall Stories

DRINK UP YUR ZIDER!

Storytelling used to take place during the long winter months when it was too dark to work in the fields. These yarns were passed between farmers either in the warmth of their homes or the local pub and one in particular was repeated many times, being that of a lad who went to fetch some cider for his boss. In true Devonian vernacular it goes something like this:

The gaffer said to the boy, 'Go to pub and get quart of zider'. The lad went off across the field towards the stile, but as he climbed over he knocked the jug and broke it. With only the handle in his hand he continued to the pub where the landlord asked him, 'What do 'e want?'

'Two pints of zider for t' boss,' the boy replied.

The landlord enquired, 'Where be going to put zider then?'

'In't jug,' the boy said, lifting the handle.

'But you've only got 'andle!' the landlord exclaimed.

The boy took off his trilby hat and turning it over indicated, 'In yer.'

The landlord raised his eyebrows somewhat but did as he was bid. Some cider was left so he asked, 'Where be going to put rest?'

Turning the hat over, the boy again pointed, 'In yer!'

The lad now walked back very carefully so as not to spill a drop. On arrival his boss asked, 'Where be me zider?'

The boy held out his hat. On looking at the hat his gaffer asked, 'But where be rest of zider?'

The boy smiled and, turning the hat over, replied, 'In yer!'

A PRICKLY SITUATION

At the end of a busy market day in Totnes, farmers who had more than their fill of cider often fell asleep in the pub, whereupon their less inebriated friends would carry them out and prop them up in their carts. Then, patting the ponies on their rumps, they sent their mates trotting over the bridge towards Paignton and home. A pretty reliable arrangement one would have thought, except for the day when one farmer's pony decided to stop at the roadside for some light refreshment. The abrupt change of direction caused the farmer to wake up and, seeing a massive shape looming up in front of him and thinking he was about to be attacked, lashed out only to find himself in the arms of a gigantic thistle!

Starkey, Knight & Ford brewery in Princes Street. (*Peggy Parnell*)

THREE STRONG MEN

At least twice a day horses and cattle would be taken to the stone water trough in Colley End for a drink and Paigntonians, like the animals, also needed that occasional drink! A local character called Tug, who worked for the local council, regularly popped into the Victoria pub for a quickie, but one cold winter's evening, having had a jar too many, slipped on the cobbles outside and fell flat on his back. At that precise moment it was his misfortune that the local bobby happened by and, in no uncertain voice, bellowed 'Get up!'

Came a feeble voice, 'Can't, three strong men are holding me down.'

'And whooooo', drawled the bobby, 'are the three men?'

Tug weakly replied, 'Starkey, Knight and Ford!'

LUNCH BREAK

A local plumber and his apprentice were having their break while carrying out a job in Roundham. The lady of the house offered the plumber a napkin. 'Thank you very much,' said the plumber. The lady turned to the apprentice and asked, 'Would you like one?'

The apprentice replied, 'If he can eat one, so can I!'

HELPFUL CITIZEN

A convict had escaped from Princetown prison and police were checking vehicles across the moor. Leo Head had just been watching a dairy herd and, on seeing a nearby policeman, got off his bike and asked, 'Would you like to search my saddlebag?'

CHAPTER THREE

The Legend of Coverdale Tower

The question has to be asked, why did nineteenth-century Paigntonians refer to the old tower in Bishop's Place as the 'Coverdale Tower'? Was it perhaps a figment of their imagination, or a desire to promote their small farming town as a place of some importance by attaching a well-known historical name to a building that once belonged to the Bishops of Exeter, but then why particularly Miles Coverdale? Or was there perhaps an element of truth in what the locals were saying? Unfortunately 'word of mouth' is not sufficient and now, regrettably with lack of evidence to back up their story, the connection with Miles Coverdale and the fine old watchtower has been dropped, although until quite recently Paigntonians remained resolute that he lived in the tower and while there translated and corrected Tyndale's English Bible, so much so they even named a road, several houses and a business after him.

Today Coverdale's connection with the old tower is considered highly unlikely, as it is well known he spent considerable periods abroad while rewriting Tyndale's work. But if the legend is correct and he did use the tower in 1535, one must ask why was he in the tower when the palace was still in existence and why Paignton. Perhaps a journey back in time might throw some light on this legend.

Miles Coverdale was a child of Yorkshire parents, born it is said near Middleham in 1488, probably in a district then known as Cover-dale in the North Riding of Yorkshire. He entered Cambridge University to study philosophy and theology, was ordained as a priest at Norwich in 1514, then in 1523 entered the convent of Augustinian friars at Cambridge, where he met a prior called Robert Barnes who introduced him to the Protestant ideas of Calvin and Luther, the 'New Religion' as it was becoming known. When Barnes was tried for heresy in 1526 Coverdale assisted in his defence, then promptly left the convent of friars to give himself entirely to preaching. Coverdale and Barnes had researched the works of Augustine, which led them to the Bible. Having made a thorough study of the scriptures they encouraged many other students and ministers of the church to look more deeply into Christianity and Biblical theology. At Thomas More's house Coverdale met Thomas Cromwell who became a good friend and supporter. He also became involved in a secret group that met at the White

Horse Tavern, Cambridge, where many theological questions were discussed; because of their connections with the new Protestant thinking that was sweeping across Europe, this tavern was given the code name Germany. In 1528 Coverdale was informed against and because he was in danger of being burnt for heresy he quickly left for Europe, where he met and listened first hand to those two eminent reformers Martin Luther and John Calvin. In Hamburg he arranged a meeting with Tyndale but owing to an accident his letter was delayed. However, they did meet eventually and together worked on the Old Testament.

Because Luther's writings were suppressed in England in 1525, Tyndale's first English translation of the New Testament was done secretly in Hamburg and printed in Worms in 1526. It is said this Bible, initially 15,000 copies, was smuggled into England in bales of merchandise, sold very cheaply and proved very popular throughout the country. But the convocation (an assembly of English bishops) was none too happy with the problems that might follow this publication so the Mayor of London, Cuthbert Tonsall, bought up every copy and had the lot burnt. With the money gained from this, Tyndale ran another edition, but unfortunately Thomas More exposed the inaccuracies in his new translation. In fact the convocation had no desire to withhold the scriptures from the public. Their only wish was to prevent errors being printed. When it became clear that the public would not be satisfied without an English version of the Bible, the convocation recommended that the bishops should make a new translation that could be issued on their authority. Meanwhile several private concerns had started publishing and circulating their own versions of the Bible – the first was by Thomas Cromwell, the king's vice-regent and Coverdale's friend. The many variations in these editions strongly indicated a need for a more careful and scholarly rendering. Cromwell, having already convinced Henry VIII of the need for an official English Bible, invited Coverdale to edit and correct Tyndale's inaccuracies, but this still didn't meet with the approval of the convocation or the crown; even so, Coverdale's corrected version of Tyndale's Bible was eventually completed and under Thomas Cromwell's protection an English printer published it on 4 October 1535. The finished copies duly appeared in the market place and have ever since been considered the first English Bible. Subsequently more revisions and translations were produced, apparently with the assistance of Coverdale, one in Paris in 1540 becoming known as 'Cranmer's' or the 'Great Bible'.

From 1543 to 1547, the year in which Henry VIII died, Coverdale was travelling on the Continent. Returning to England in 1547, he stayed at Windsor Castle where the Windsor Commission was preparing the first Book of Common Prayer. But he was soon to discover the church and its clergy were in turmoil. In fact it was total chaos, with the highest officers of the realm wantonly destroying and appropriating holy things, while people availed themselves of coffins to use as horse-troughs and adapting altar cloths, vestments and Eucharist vessels for domestic purposes. According to the *English Church History* (1904) 'it was harvest time for thieves and high holiday for the profane'. Things went from bad to worse when episcopal manors were seized through a system of forced exchanges, thus impoverishing the sees, incomes were withheld from vicars and the whole thing became a regular plan to defraud the episcopate; but young King Edward VI soon put a stop to these unlawful activities.

Before Coverdale was sent down to Devon in 1549 as chaplain to Lord Russell to help quieten the Prayer Book rebellion, he had been commissioned to prosecute those who infringed the new Book of Common Prayer, and at the same time he also preached at the penance of some Anabaptists. Immediately following this incident, which had occurred on the second Sunday in Lent, Coverdale's powerful preaching caused the sacrament at the high altar of St Paul's in London to be pulled down. So, as can be seen, Miles Coverdale was as much a rebel against the establishment as anyone else and certainly did his best to turn the hearts of the rebels with his persuasive preaching. Indeed he was one of the most effective preachers of his time. For all this he was highly thought of at court and was often at Windsor Castle. In 1550 he was made suffragan bishop in the diocese of Exeter; he also became Queen Catherine Parr's almoner and chaplain to Edward VI. In 1551, on the enforced retirement and recommendation of Bishop Voysey, who had reached an almost mythical age of around 100, Miles Coverdale was appointed Bishop of Exeter, the see at this time included Devon and Cornwall.

Edward VI's recent Act of Parliament ended the customary method of appointing bishops, who now had to be consecrated on the authority of royal letters patent. The Act also provided that all episcopal acts of jurisdiction should be done in the king's name and that a bishop's office would now only be tenable at the king's pleasure instead of for life, which meant any obstructive bishop could be quickly dismissed. On the king's authority Miles Coverdale was thus consecrated on 14 August 1551 by Archbishop Cranmer at Croydon instead of in Exeter Cathedral. On taking up his post in Exeter, following his first sermon on the new faith, two attempts were made to poison him. Coverdale was also horrified to discover the cathedral had been virtually stripped clean. According to *The Lives of the Bishops of Exeter* (published in Exeter in 1861 by the Revd George Oliver), on 20 December 1551 'Coverdale ordained a number of deacons and on 1 January 1552 he ordained on the same day a deacon and a priest in the chapel of his palace, but all other ordinations were conducted in his cathedral.' What is meant by this phrase is not quite clear. Was the palace being referred to the one at Exeter or one of the other fourteen throughout the diocese? It is said that of all Bishop Voysey's palaces only three remained intact at his retirement and one surely must have been Exeter. On the other hand, since Bishop Quivil's time (1280-91) the palace at Paignton, having had close connections with the Precentor of Exeter Cathedral and although in need of considerable repair was still in existence in 1553 having escaped seizure by the forced exchange system. It is known the chapel of St Mary's at Paignton had been used for many ordinations and ecclesiastical meetings over the years.

The report on the *Lives of the Bishops of Exeter* also states that under the new juristic powers Coverdale, apart from trying to maintain his position in the cathedral, must have found it very painful having to join the king's commission, which consisted of two knights, Sir Peter Carewe and Sir Thomas Denys, the mayor of Exeter and an alderman (a mayor's assistant), and having to insist that his own dean and chapter appear before the commission in his palace on 30 September 1552 to answer questions relating to the cathedral's jewels, plate and other ornaments, which may have had something to do with the pilfering that had being going on in the cathedral. Again the text does not state which palace, so one presumes it to be Exeter. However, Sir Peter Carewe and Sir Thomas Denys were two well-known names associated with the manor of Paignton in both the sixteenth and seventeenth centuries and, as already mentioned, the Palace Chapel of St Mary had been used for many episcopal meetings before the reformation, so was it perhaps here that this meeting took place?

A lithograph showing the remains of the Bishop's Palace at Paignton. By the late eighteenth century there was still a considerable amount of the chapel left. (*Peggy Parnell*)

In 1545 Henry VIII entrusted Thomas Speke with the Manor of Paignton, which he held until Queen Mary bestowed it on Lord Pembroke in 1557. In an old tourist book of Torbay from the early twentieth century there was a line that read, 'Coverdale loved his palace of Paignton.' Certainly he had two years as bishop during Speke's tenure when he could have visited the palace, even though it is said the building had been officially closed six years earlier in 1547.

Soon after young Edward VI ascended the throne he started to take control and was aghast, among many other improprieties, at the way episcopal manors were being seized and forcibly exchanged. He did much to reinstate what he could, which might account for the fact that the palace buildings remained in Speke's hands until 1553. However, the Pembroke survey of 1566 noted that in 1553 a large building called the Great Stable, although in need of repair, was still habitable and was indentured to a Richard Churchward. The survey also mentioned a house nearby which Emma Bennett had moved into. So it would seem that parts of the old palace were still fit for human habitation in 1553 and had not yet been totally disposed of along with other episcopal manors. When Queen Mary came to the throne she did her best to reinstate many ecclesiastical buildings, but by this time the Paignton Palace was being transferred to various people, perhaps before the Queen could put a stop to their disposal. There is little doubt that what was written in Pembroke's Survey is correct, which means Coverdale could have stayed in the palace between 1551 and 1553. But in 1553, on becoming Queen, Mary deprived Coverdale of his bishopric and had him imprisoned (where has not been discovered) and promptly restored John Voysey as bishop, despite his great age. Coverdale remained in prison for two and a half years. When imprisoned on 1 September 1553 he had many accusations made against him, but really it was his Calvinistic leanings and his marriage – unlawful according to the Catholic Church – that Queen Mary was opposed to, and because of this she seriously considered having him executed.

An old tourist book on south Devon by Hanniford and Rowe mentions that 'Coverdale possibly occupied the tower in 1535', but they were doubtful about the date. Hanniford and Rowe were quite right to question this for if Coverdale did use the tower, as many claimed he did, then the dates that have been quoted do not tie up, whereas if it had been 1553 it could well mean this is where he was imprisoned. Certainly it was just the sort of place Queen Mary might have chosen for someone like Coverdale, for with him being the son of an ordinary Yorkshire man she would not have placed him under house arrest in the home of a nobleman, and neither, as he was a man of the cloth (a priest), would she have placed him in a common prison.

As it so happened public feeling in the West Country was still strongly Papist and Coverdale, despite the fact that he was a good man and a blameless bishop, was not popular with the ordinary people who could not accept him because he preached the Gospel in English, which made him an enemy of the Papist cause, and also because he had broken the Sixth Article of Celibacy and married. These facts plus the strong Catholic support in Paignton might well have encouraged Queen Mary to consider this a pretty safe place to incarcerate such a wayward bishop, particularly as Canon Lawson, vicar of the nearby parish church, was a serious opponent to Calvinism and the new Protestant faith. This, together with the general public feeling, and the bitter animosity between these two men, meant there would have been little hope of escape for Coverdale. If Queen Mary was looking for a suitable person to place Coverdale under house arrest, then no one could have been better than Canon Lawson who had a robust tower on his doorstep!

Wherever Miles Coverdale's place of imprisonment was, it is said he was examined rigorously by his inquisitors and was constantly in peril of his life, but strangely came to no harm. His safekeeping is attributed to his wife's connections with King Christian III of Denmark, who through her brother-in-law's intervention on his behalf, pleaded with Queen Mary who was related to King Christian's family. Eventually in 1555, with a proper Act of Parliament, Coverdale was granted free passage to Denmark with bags, baggage and servants, with his wife, it is said, masquerading as one of the servants. In this way Coverdale joined the hundreds of people fleeing England to eventually arrive safely in Denmark with his wife and family. While in Denmark he busied himself translating into English Calvin's treatise on the Eucharist and declined King Christian III's kind offer of a living in Denmark; instead he travelled around considerably, returning to England in 1559 for the last time when he was offered back his bishopric, but refused on the grounds of conscientious objections over his 'uncanonical' method of appointment and his refusal to wear episcopal vestments. He decided instead to take the living of St Magnus the Martyr near St Paul's in London. But the problems which led to his resignation in 1566 still besieged him and although he only preached occasionally he always attracted a large audience. Two years later, in February 1568, he died. Many years later in 1919 Edward VI's letters patent, granting Coverdale's appointment to the bishopric of Exeter, were discovered in Crediton.

From all that has been written it is obvious Coverdale lived in turbulent times, constantly in danger of his life. However, there must have been some foundation to the story of his connection with the Bishop's Tower in Paignton for his name to be associated with it for so many centuries. Here it is worth quoting an extract from a reading by W.G. Couldrey on 21 June 1932:

The existing tower is known as 'Coverdale Tower' and there is a persistent legend that Miles Coverdale, when Bishop of Exeter, used the room on the first floor of this building as a study, and wrote many of his works there. Many Paigntonians are of the opinion that he translated the Bible from Hebrew and Greek in this tower, but as his translation was printed in 1535, and he was appointed Bishop in 1551, this clearly is an error.

Couldrey was, of course, quite right; this extract along with other known writings about Coverdale and the tower all indicate that the dates do not make sense. But why don't they make sense?

The Bishop's/Coverdale Tower from the west. (*Frank Pearce*, The Book of Paignton, *Halsgrove, 2001*)

In the early sixteenth century the most important date embedded in the minds of people would have been the year 1535 when Coverdale's translation of the Bible into English was published. Another important event, particularly for the staunch Catholic Paigntonians, would have been 1553 when Miles Coverdale was imprisoned.

Even though these two events were eighteen years apart, later generations, unaware of Coverdale's many works, on hearing the story of him writing in the tower may have confused his celebrated translation of the 1535 Bible with the date of his imprisonment, 1553, perhaps thinking they were one and the same incident. This could simply have been because news of events were passed on by word of mouth. As later generations may well have been unaware of his numerous works, they could have confused the date of his writing in the tower with his earlier translation of the Bible. So is it possible, with the dates so very similar, that successive generations inverted 1553 and 1535. If this is what happened then the legend of Coverdale's Tower falls into place.

Unfortunately written records that could substantiate these theories are few and far between. The only possibility lies in the tower itself, which is presently (2006) being refurbished with lottery funding. It is hoped that the archaeologist may find something that will support the story of Coverdale's connection with the tower or at least throw some light on this ancient legend.

RUINS REVEAL ALL

Some 1713 deeds describe what the old Bishop's Palace ruins, still in existence on the corner of Palace Place by the parish church, were like at that time. The document also describes the area around and refers to it as:

> All that toft, being formerly a spacious Mansion House, called the Palace of Paignton together with the gatehouse and the little room adjoining called the 'dark house' or 'porter's lodge' converted into two ground rooms and the barn etc., belonging. Also two acres of land laying within the scyte of the said palace and converted into an orchard with three closes called the Gerstons otherwise the Garstons and which premises are adjoined the churchyard and more formerly, the inheritance of John Martyn of Cockington.
>
> (*The Oldenburg*, E. Britton)

The three 'closes' mentioned above can clearly be seen on the 1840 tithe map (see p. 4) as 'Gurstons', formerly 'gars tun' meaning the grass farm; probably grazing land for the bishop's horses.

Excavations carried out on behalf of the Paignton Preservation and Local History Society, funded by the Heritage Lottery Fund, have at long last revealed the history of a Grade II listed site, known for many years as St Mary's Chapel. Except for the nineteenth- and twentieth-century level finds of clay pipes and discarded bottles, what came to light was quite unexpected, for the excavation revealed this building was not necessarily a chapel but more likely a lodging house for visiting clergy, dating from between the thirteenth and fourteenth

Above: An eighteenth-century lithograph of St Mary's Chapel and the old preacher's cross, minus its lantern top. (*Peggy Parnell*)

Right: This is one side of a four-panel cross found in the grounds of Churston Church near Paignton. (*Peggy Parnell*)

centuries. Work on the north side of the site quickly exposed the remains of a garderobe block with four garderobes (toilets), two on the ground floor and two immediately above, all of which would have had wooden planking with suitable holes cut out. The contents would have dropped straight down into the Bishop's culvert, a semicircular bricked outlet (still visible) that flowed out under today's modern town, towards the marshes and sea beyond. In the east wall, just above the culvert, are traces of a further pair of wooden seats at ground level, which also discharged directly into the culvert.

A fourteenth-century doorjamb was discovered on the south side of the site. Today this doorway leads under the church path, and surviving patches of plaster on the wall along this pathway clearly indicate this was once the interior of the Bishop's Palace. In the central area of this site a substantial pit was uncovered, considered large enough to take a pillar that could have supported a heavy floor above. However, in the whole site only a few architectural fragments were found, including four pieces of medieval floor tile, the first to be recorded in Paignton.

Site of archaeological dig in 2004. (*Peggy Parnell*)

This work on the part of the Paignton Preservation and Local History Society won them the first ever HLF Heritage Heroes Award in the Buildings and Monuments category, presented at Powderham Castle on 30 March 2005. The society has since refurbished the Bishop/Coverdale Tower – the work funded by the Heritage Lottery Fund.

CHAPTER FOUR

Animals Great & Small

ELEPHANTS ON PARADE

Councillor George Spear, a rotund little chap with a ruddy complexion and a distinctive Devonian accent, was responsible for the organisation of the annual Paignton Carnival. In the summer of 1938 he busied himself setting up the various floats in Palace Avenue. As part of the parade he had borrowed two elephants from Paignton Zoo. Knowing he wouldn't have time for any lunch George had slipped a couple of apples into his pocket before leaving home, but became so involved in his preparations he clean forgot about them. During the morning George noticed the two elephants were getting rather too friendly for comfort so kept edging away until, to the amusement of onlookers, he found himself being chased around the park by them! The quicker he moved the quicker they followed. George, bless his heart, was totally unaware it was the apples they wanted, not him!

George Spear was a very popular chairman of the Paignton Urban District Council and one of his favourite quotations in his local speeches was 'It's a hard life, lucky if you can get out of it alive!'

WHAT THE TRAINS BROUGHT IN

Once the railway arrived in Paignton the trains brought in a constant supply of livestock for the farmers, as well as animals destined for Mr Whitley's Paignton Zoo. One in particular was an elephant, too big for the Whitley Estate transport, so his keeper decided to walk him through the town!

Big containers housing exotic animals were quite common, but one in particular was a crate labelled 'Beware Live Bear', which caused considerable problems for the station staff when the base of the crate collapsed. How on earth were they going to transport such a huge animal all the way to the zoo? The problem was eventually solved by fitting two long poles on either side of the crate. In true pallbearers' fashion the staff gently lifted the crate leaving the faulty floor and Bruno's feet firmly on the platform. After making sure they had secured the beast at all four corners of his crate, the entourage moved slowly through the town. Shops emptied as customers and staff ran out to witness the strange spectacle of a huge crate with four furry feet padding up Victoria Street! (Jack Baker, extract from *Chimps, Chumps & Elephants*, 1988)

SIX O'CLOCK IN THE MORNING

At 6 o'clock on a freezing cold morning there was a loud banging on my front door. Who the devil could it be at such an ungodly hour? Staggering down the stairs half asleep I slipped the chain off and opened the front door. On the doorstep, to my amazement, were three burly men. I gasped and with a quick intake of breath, fearful of what might happen, managed to stammer 'W-what do you want?'

The short plump man nearest the door spoke first, 'May we come through to your back garden?'

My face must have registered a strange expression. 'My back garden?' I gulped.

'Oh! It's all right sir,' the plump man said reassuringly, 'We're from the BBC and at some time in the night a gibbon escaped from Paignton Zoo. Apparently the lake froze and allowed him to cross from his island residence and he is now sitting contentedly on your roof!'

THE DONKEY MAN

An old thatched cottage which once stood between Higher Polsham Road and West Hill was known to older Paigntonians as 'Donkey Daniels' house, so named because the owner ran donkey rides on the sands. The first Donkey Daniels was a man with an enormously bushy beard that covered his face, and in addition to his donkey business he also hired out bath-chairs, advertising them as 'The cheapest means

Donkey Daniels taking on new rides under Paignton Pier. (*Totnes Images*)

The Daniels' home, Southfield Road, Paignton. (*Frank Pearce*, The Book of Paignton, *Halsgrove, 2001*)

The type of contraption Donkey Daniels would have used. (*Peggy Parnell*)

of transport to be had with adequate shelter from rain and sun'. In these chairs he would take ladies for a ride along the prom or anywhere else they so requested. The system was that Madam would take the handle and old Donkey Daniels would push.

On one of these occasions he brought a lady to the first Catholic church in Colley End. Parking the chair outside he sat in it and waited while she went to mass. After the service the priest, standing at the top of the steps seeing his congregation out, spotted the strange contraption with the white-bearded man sitting in it. Being new to the church he had no idea who it was and probably had never seen anything like the bath-chair contraption before. Looking down at a small lad standing next to him, the priest asked 'Who is the poor old man in the chair? We must help him.'

The youngster grinned, 'Oh, that's only Donkey Daniels!'

Donkey Daniels had a son, a character in his own right who eventually took over the donkey rides along Paignton's esplanade. Donkey Daniels junior cared little for his appearance, but had a delightful little wife. For a time they lived with Donkey Daniels senior in his thatched cottage opposite the old tollhouse (near the present police station) before the cottage was eventually removed for road widening. While there the couple had a son and when he was old enough they sent him to the Catholic school in Colley End, asking if someone would be kind enough to see their little boy home each afternoon. The same young lad who told the priest about old Donkey Daniels was approached, and although only ten years of age he never forgot what a sweet lady Mrs Daniels was and couldn't get over the difference between husband and wife, with him being such a rugged and unkempt character and she so neat and tidy. However, their son grew up to be a real gentleman and, although interested in Dartmoor ponies, had no interest in his father's and grandfather's business – so the donkey rides disappeared. Now, at long last, although no longer belonging to the Daniels family, the donkeys have returned to the seafront, this time without their straw hats as they now have a smart gazebo on the Green giving them protection from the hot sun and pouring rain. (Extract from Michael Adams' *Memoirs*, 2002)

A DONKEY RIDE

The driver and clippie of the No. 12 Brixham bus were sitting on a seat at the Goodrington bus stop, beside their double-decker bus. Donkey Daniels was walking one of his donkeys towards Goodrington beach, having just finished a bevy of cider for his lunch, when he had an inspiration. The clippie and driver quietly finished their lunch and returned to the bus to discover Donkey Daniels on the bus with one of his four-footed friends! No matter how they tried they could not get the animal off and in the end, in sheer desperation, took the bus back to the depot where piece by piece they took the inside apart before the poor animal could be released.

PADDING FEET

At four o'clock one morning a well-known Paignton dairyman, on his way through Well Street to collect his van from a garage in Cecil Road, became aware of someone, or something, following him. 'Oh heck!' he gulped, suddenly remembering that a leopard had reportedly escaped from Paignton Zoo. Instantly the hair on his body sprang into the vertical and rather than look behind him he began to walk quicker, but the faster he walked the faster that something followed him. Arriving at his garage he leapt inside and secured the door. Only then did he dare look through a crack to discover the 'leopard' was an Alsatian dog!

HAPPY HENS

Winner Street in the early 1920s had altered very little since the gentlemen's houses were built on the rise at the west end junction of Winner Street, with gates and gardens that reached down to the pavement below. One day a lad and his father went to collect a table from one of the houses situated above Bailey's Emporium (recently Pot Black). Passing through the iron gate, they climbed the steep steps that curved towards the house and on through a garden choked with overgrown trees and shrubs from which emerged a large number of cats begging for attention. An old lady who lived there alone opened the door. On entering the house the sight and smell that greeted them was unbelievable, for happily perched on the banister rails were dozens of hens, the stairs beneath them caked in droppings! (Extract from Michael Adams' *Memoirs*, 2002)

GENTLE GIANTS AND LITTLE BOWS

An Exeter company of wine merchants called Carr & Quick Ltd eventually bought both premises belonging to the Waycott brothers in Winner Street, and in the early twentieth century demolished the lot and rebuilt a block of flats over two shops, with a loading bay in between. The bay is used today as an extension to a carpet shop, but in those days anyone who happened to walk along the pavement during Regatta or Carnival Week might well have witnessed the wine merchants' magnificent dray horses emerging from this loading bay. With manes neatly tied in little bows and their feathers (leg hair) groomed to perfection and dressed overall in colourful rosettes, shining brasses and jingling bells, they were a truly magnificent sight. As a small child I was equally awe-struck by the occasional sight of these gentle giants trotting majestically through the streets pulling heavy barrels of beer and cider, their huge hoofs hitting the ground in a rhythmic thud, thud, thud.

A POCKET FULL OF WRIGGLIES

In 1787 ideas considered by a frustrated brewer, an ambitious postman and a redundant soap boiler brought about the family business of Greenall-Whitley. By 1892 Mr Edward Whitley was a man well loved by the people of Liverpool; he was a solicitor, great churchman, keen political rival and friend of William Gladstone, mayor and brewery baron, from which he made his fortune.

Edward Whitley died at the age of sixty-seven leaving his wife Eleanor Whitley with a young family of three boys and one girl. Fortunately she was a trained schoolmistress, which helped her control the family. She was a true Victorian lady with lace cap and black dress in the style of Queen Victoria herself. Although her children descended from a long line of solicitors they had a very different outlook on life, being much more interested in nature and the world around them. So Mrs Whitley came to the conclusion that Liverpool, with its dockland and factories, was no place for a young adolescent family to grow up and in 1904 moved family and home into the country.

Why Devon and why Paignton in particular is not known. Perhaps it was because she had spent her honeymoon here and knew about a grand house called Primley with its large grounds which reached almost to the sea. Whatever the reason, the family and their belongings duly arrived in Paignton via the Great Western Railway, known to the locals as God's Wonderful Railway, and were greeted by their head coachman, a distinctive figure with a cockaded top hat and 'mutton-chop' whiskers who, together with the household retainers, had travelled ahead to prepare their new home at Primley House.

It must have been quite something for the three boys and their sister to find themselves in a country environment with an uninterrupted view of the sea and livestock all around them, add then to learn that the ancient manor-town of Paignton, dating from before 1066 rivalled in age that of Liverpool. They must have been thrilled at setting their eyes on the attractive white mansion nestling on

The southerly aspect of Primley House. (*Peggy Parnell*)

Primley Hill with its magnificent stairway and the name denoting 'a meadow on the edge of woodland facing the sunrise'.

Primley had recently been the home of a family called Belfield who acquired the property through marriage sometime in the eighteenth century, their ancestors having fled to the south during the religious purge by Henry VIII. It is said the very last member of this family disappeared mysteriously, a story yet to be researched.

Just imagine the three Whitley boys in their Victorian white starched collars and flat pancake caps exploring the stables, kennels and farm buildings. What surprises they must have discovered, particularly young Herbert who would have quickly filled his pockets with as many life forms as he could find. As a small boy his mother had bought him a pair of canaries, and with this memory in mind he would have made straight for the pigeon house to organise the blues from the blacks, about which he knew everything.

Herbert spent many happy hours among the sixteen greenhouses where his love for animals and plants developed. A few years later brother William graduated with honours from Bromsgrove School and joined the cavalry at Sandhurst, but after falling through a stable skylight was discharged and decided farming was more to his liking. Herbert, on the other hand, being more interested in the feathered world, left Bromsgrove School for an agricultural course at Cambridge. Eventually it was decided the two brothers, Herbert and William, should run the Primley estate together. This meant a lot of hard work and young Herbert had to leave his jungle on the doorstep to concentrate on their new business of W. & H. Whitley. Twenty years later, after a series of events and two world wars, the little boy with livestock and seedlings in his pocket found himself in Clennon Valley organising his life's dream, known today as the Paignton Zoological and Botanical Gardens.

When Herbert Whitley's old zoo truck decided to have one of its regular punctures nearby his friend's home, Herbert walked the few yards down the road to the house and knocked on the door. The butler answered and Herbert, in as few words as possible, asked if he could use the phone. The butler viewed the disgusting tramp standing on the doorstep and went immediately to his master who instructed him to pass the phone out through the window. On returning home Herbert rang his friend to congratulate him on his choice of butler, who had displayed such a high standard of care when dealing with scruffy individuals!

Cows! Cows! Cows!

From time immemorial Paignton was involved in agricultural and animal husbandry. The period between the two world wars saw farm animals constantly being transported across Devon. With the arrival of the GWR in 1859 livestock was transported in and out of Paignton in ever increasing numbers and loaded off trucks into Brunel's goods yard (now the ticket office). They were then herded through Victoria Street into Palace Avenue and Winner Street, while others were taken through Hyde Road, up Church Street into a resting area behind the Crown & Anchor. Others were taken to special areas such as the Co-operative Society's

Kingwell's state of the art shop opposite the opening into the new Palace Trading Estate, now Palace Avenue. (*T. Moss*)

slaughterhouses in Great Parks and Luscombe Lane and well-known butchers such as Palk, Williams and Ginn who stored their cattle behind the Pumping Station in Clennon Valley.

Following the arrival of Brunel's railway, butcher's shops started to abound and one in particular stood where Palace Avenue meets Winner Street. This particular shop belonged to a butcher called Kingwell whose house opposite stood just where the developers needed to open up an entrance into Paignton's new business estate. It must have been a shock when he learnt his lovely home was to be demolished, but this enterprising man quickly turned a disadvantage to an advantage and agreed to his property being pulled down providing he was adequately compensated, an action that enabled him to transform his shop into a 'state of the art' butchery with expensive marble slabs, white tiles with blue animal motifs, brass fittings and the very latest gas lighting. Next to Kingwell's refurbished shop, a pair of heavy doors led into an old court farm where, some years later, under the entrance arch a little showroom of ornamental fish was installed, but during Kingwell's time these doors were the entrance to a court farm where he had a small slaughterhouse. This was quite normal practice in the days before deep-freezers, which enabled butchers to keep their stocks freshly to hand.

Kingwell's stock always arrived confused after the long train journey from the Newton Abbot and Totnes markets and that last lap through the town was more than they could endure, so much so that on reaching the heavy double doors and catching the whiff of death they would put their noses down and refuse to enter.

The best known of these slaughter yards and possibly the oldest one in Paignton was at the rear of the seventeenth-century Crown & Anchor coaching inn, where Prince William of Orange stayed overnight en route to London. Here at the rear of the inn cattle were rested in a shed, fed and watered until called to the 'bar', so to speak! By the nineteenth century some buildings at the side of this slaughterhouse appear to have been used in the process of butchering, for during the recent conversions of Crown & Anchor Way it was discovered that one of the ground-floor rooms had twenty-four heavy iron ceiling hooks, almost certainly used for hanging and stripping carcasses.

Butchery and slaughtering in particular became big business in Paignton, to the extent that some butchers even carried out their own dressing. One in particular was Pook Bros in Church Street who had two iron hooks, one on each side of the shop entrance, where, to the repugnance of their customers, Ginger Hooper would sever the carcass' in half!

Pook Bros, situated on the site of the old Crown & Anchor coaching inn. (*From Peter Tully's* Pictures of Paignton Part II, *Obelisk, 1992*)

There were numerous slaughterhouses in Paignton and one was off Colley End Road near the Greebys (spelt Greybey in the 1840s). Here stood three cottages overlooking a farm. In the end cottage lived a tiny little man who made baskets and repaired cane chairs.

On Wednesday afternoons during the Second World War a local herdsman named Cyril Clark helped to unload livestock into Paignton's goods yard then drive the cattle 'on the hoof' up Hyde Road to the various slaughter yards. One day he made a delivery to a particular field near the Greebys where certain cattle were grassed-out before slaughter. Here a bull, perhaps sensing death, went berserk and the farmer, unable to control it, sought the help of the police to calm the beast down. The poor animal fought for his life, but lost in the end when a bullet found its mark.

Another well-known butcher's shop was Foale's Corner, now Tesco. This family business owned a field in Shorton Lane where their young stock was kept ready for slaughter. In this field the farmer kept an old galvanised bath for collecting rainwater and when the bath was dry he would take the animals to the stone trough in Colley End. However, by the time they reached the old tollhouse at the bottom of Shorton Lane they would get restless and separate. A little further on and the animals were all but stampeding, so astride his pony the farmer would round them up. Watching the bandy-legged farmer with keen interest, the local lads saw him as him as a real Wild West cowboy straight out of the 'flicks'. On reaching the water trough the farmer sometimes found other herds already there, and with so many animals drinking at the same time many cows wandered off until the greedy ones had had their fill. Early in the twentieth century a few cars began to appear and if one was unfortunate enough to arrive at drinking time the cattle, having no respect for such a strange animal, would give it a good old nudge! Just imagine a

Devon Reds. (*Peggy Parnell*)

This trough in Colley End was later replaced by an elegant iron fountain for the use of man and beast. (*Frank Pearce,* Torbay The Golden Years, *Halsgrove, 2002*)

huge crowd of cows and all their droppings with a vintage car stuck in the middle. Eventually the various livestock were sorted out, rounded up and driven back to their respective fields, leaving Colley End looking like a typical farmyard.

Like all the farmers on the surrounding hills one farmer named Mitchell would drive his cows up and down twice a day to his milking parlour in Well Street, with his 'boss' cow always leading off, and when all were milked she would be the first out leading the herd back up Marldon Hill, but not before stopping for a drink at the old stone trough in Colley End. The local lads knew all these cows by name and could tell many a tale about the numerous dairymen shuttling their herds to and fro between the meadows flanking Marldon Hill; and during a good summer in the nearby fields they often heard a corncrake (a bird associated with hay or corn) constantly crying out. In those days it was customary for a dairy farmer to pay young boys a small sum of money to shut his parlour gate. One lad in particular named Michael Adams recalls being offered 1d to do just this and often followed farmer Mitchell driving his cows down the hill to his milking parlour in Well Street, which was opposite the old quarry where Michael's father stabled his horse. This quarry, so Michael was told, was the one used by the bishops when building the medieval palace as well as for successive repairs on the parish church. Eventually the quarry and stables became a garage workshop and latterly modern homes. (Extract from Michael Adams' *Memoirs,* 2002)

CHAPTER FIVE

Odd Characters

AS BLACK AS CAN BE

A little way up Colley End once stood three old houses, the foundations of which were 3ft below road level, which rather suggests they could be several hundreds of years old. In one of these cottages there lived an old man called Mr Shute, reputed to have been an old trawler-man; certainly his hands and face were as sunburnt as could be and as a small child I mistakenly thought he was dirty. He certainly was a source of amusement to many a passer-by for periodically he would tie toy army trucks onto the end of a stick and dangle them out of his bedroom window. Old Mr Shute often stood outside his front door leaning on the railings, chewing 'baccy and spitting it onto the road, so much that the area became blackened with tobacco stains. Next door, standing in a cherry orchard, was once a similar house, now a group of maisonettes. One day a workman carrying out repairs in this house happened to say something derogatory about the strange old man next door, when suddenly a fellow worker looked up and said, 'That's my grandpa, watch it!'

THE LITTLE WOODEN HOUSE

A local personality named Michael Adams used to enjoy a walk from Goodrington up the hill to Three Beaches, where turning left he made his way over the stone railway bridge onto the headland and an area he called White Horse Cove. From here he would wander down to one of the three coves, although sometimes he turned left and stopped at the cliff edge to look at some hydrangeas growing on a ledge below here, washed by the sea's spray, stood a little wooden house, the home of an extraordinary and highly intelligent man named Elbert Foster. Elbert was a recluse and young Michael remembered vividly how strangely he dressed, for he always wore an ordinary blue serge suit with trousers that appeared to be cut off at the knees, heavy boots and stockings to the knees! By contrast his sister-in-law Emmy was a charming lady married to Elbert's brother Roland Foster, both highly respected members of Paignton society who lived in the large family home in Grosvenor Road. Having no children, Emmy would throw large birthday parties for her nieces and nephews, and always invited her neighbours' children.

Elbert was tall with a full bearded face and according to his great nephew, Bob LeMarchant, actually wore sandals and shorts summer and winter and not cut-off trousers as suggested by Michael. In fact he was a very hospitable man, not in the least bit intimidating; it was just his presence and strange eyes that concerned people. He was very clean and always had a boiling pot of stew over a smoky fire, so that when visitors stopped by for a chat he would offer them some. But he was a vegetarian and in those days people were suspicious about this kind of food, so family and friends politely refused, never daring to accept his kind hospitality; neither had he any seating so callers would stand first on one foot then on the other. For all this Elbert was an active member of St Andrew's Church where he was churchwarden and where he donated a silver chalice engraved by him.

For many years his little hut was of great interest to locals and tourists, but during the Second World War, because of its secluded position, the army requisitioned the ledge for a small gunnery encampment, so Elbert's little home and its contents were removed to sister Emmy's back garden in Grosvenor Road where he continued to live until he died in the early 1950s. Interestingly Emmy's sister Kate married Harry Wanless, a prolific painter from Scarborough who, it is strongly suspected, encouraged Elbert's brother Roland Foster to paint the local views of old Paignton, some of which presently hang in Oldway Mansion.

THE HERB MAN

During the 1930s and '40s Paignton had several unusual and you could even say 'odd' characters. In particular were two sisters and their brother who were often seen carrying fish frails (flat woven grass bags), which Gypsies often traded when passing through a town. The two sisters were never seen apart although their brother often went off on his own, usually onto the promenade where he would approach people with bunches of wild flowers and herbs. One day he approached an elderly lady and, being the gentleman he was, raised his hat and using his best cultured voice wished her good morning, adding 'Would you like a bunch of white heather?' To which the lady replied, 'Oh! How kind of you', but before she could say thank you he had extracted sixpence!

These people seemed to collect herbs commercially, probably picked from the local hedges and fields. Certainly they somehow made a living for they were never short of money. The two sisters, by their style of hair, hats and clothes, belonged to a generation earlier (the Edwardian period). Their brother seemed to be the one who gathered the heather, but in time he went a bit odd and started wearing skin-tight white flannels; how he got into or out of them was something of a mystery. Nobody seemed to know anything about him or his sisters, then, quite suddenly, all three vanished! (Extract from Michael Adams' *Memoirs*, 2002)

ALL IN WHITE

Another odd couple regularly seen around Paignton during the early part of the Second World War were always dressed in white whatever the time of the year. Be it summer or winter he was dressed in white flannels, shirt and jacket and she in a long white dress, white stockings, white shoes and a huge wide-brimmed white hat, the outfit completed with an ensemble of white gloves, umbrella and handbag. It was as if they had just returned from the tropics and this was their only wardrobe. Who knows, that might just have been the reason: this was wartime after all.

MISS BERRY

There was, in the late 1920s to the early 1950s, a lady who lived alone in a grand Georgian house called Coniston in Sands Road, known locally as Miss Berry. In about 1912 Miss Berry and her daughter moved to Paignton, possibly after Mr Berry died. Why they chose to come to Paignton is not known, but what is known is that Miss Berry was the daughter of the once-celebrated manufacturer of Berry's boot polish. Whatever or whoever Miss Berry may have been she was certainly renowned for her extraordinarily large and well-designed Edwardian hats resembling huge bowls of fruits and flowers, which this gracious lady wore in a very regal way whenever in town.

It is alleged that Coniston House was originally built for the daughter of a well-known local businessman named Mr Charles Bailey. The fact that he built the house is confirmed by a plaque high up on the west wall of the house which reads 'This stone was laid by Charles E. Bailey – 21 August 1801'.

Coniston House in Sands Road, now apartments. (*Peggy Parnell*)

HER FACE WAS DEAD WHITE

Mr Bailey, a rather strange and formidable character, was a prominent businessman and local councillor who added his mark to the development of Paignton. This gentleman lived in the second half of the nineteenth century and, apart from his involvement in the town's new water supply, built a number of good properties around Paignton, in particular all those buildings that sweep around Station Square, part of which is now a nightclub. Although the signboards over the buildings have long vanished, they are still grand edifices of Edwardian architecture. In addition to these establishments, Bailey also built two mini-mansions, one being the grand Edwardian building called Coniston in Sands Road, the other being Tower House which became the Marist Convent and later an independent school. He was also responsible for the buildings at the west end of Winner Street, again with windows and walls of beautifully dressed limestone blocks, topped with the ever-popular baubles and pineapples of the period. All of his buildings have the classic hallmark of two inimitable local architects, Messers Couldrey and Bridgeman.

Michael Adams, who once lived in Climsland Road, remembers that Mr Bailey would stand in the doorway of his Winner Street emporium smoking a cigar, dressed in a tweed suit of loud checks with yellow waistcoat and watch-chains going left and right across his rather large belly. To young Michael Mr Bailey's head appeared to come out of a high starched collar that seemed to be supporting his large purple face, which was covered by a huge curly moustache. Michael wasn't sure, but thought his colour was possibly due to excessive alcohol. Sometimes Bailey and his wife would stand together in the shop entrance waiting for customers, although the lad never saw anyone go in. The wife frightened Michael for her face was dead white, as if painted in whitewash, her mouth a scarlet dash and her eyelids painted black. Apparently this was the style of make-up used in the early silent films known as the 'flicks' (flickering pictures) for in those days films were only black and white, colour having yet to be invented. Perhaps, considered Michael, she was in the flicks herself.

Mr Bailey's Emporium was thought by many to be little more than a junk shop, but Michael once made a purchase there. While nosing in the shop one day he saw a great stack of books just inside the door and among them was a large book priced two pence, and as he had two pence he bought it and took it home. It was possibly an evangelical book or something, Michael wasn't sure. On returning home his mother asked him if he had bought it. 'You did? Then take it right back and say you couldn't read it and ask for your two pence back'. The lad did as he was told, but Mr Bailey retorted, 'You bought it, you've got it!'

The reason for Mr Bailey starting his two emporiums was, it is thought, a glut of blue eastern chinaware that was shipped into Paignton harbour, whether commercially or from a shipwreck is not known. Whatever Mr Bailey's business activities were, he was an entrepreneurial man who did a great deal for Paignton, but for some unknown reason, it is said, he suddenly closed everything down. But when this happened is not known.

CHAPTER SIX

A Family Saga

THE MILLERS TALE

Two families by the name of Rossiter are well known in Paignton and both can trace a common ancestry to around 1216, at which time they moved among the highest levels of society. Although their English origin was in a place called 'Rocester' in Lincolnshire, they actually came over with the Norman Conquest and for their services to William I were granted land in Ireland where a Robert Rosseter claimed advowson to a vacant living there in 1357.

The earliest recorded Rossiter in Paignton was christened in St John's parish church in 1684, but his son Richard was born in Wexford, Ireland, in 1710. Why would a Rossiter born in Ireland in 1710 want to come to Paignton in 1740? The answer could be the father, who possibly remained a practising Catholic and with all the restrictions imposed on English Catholics at this time had decided to join his Catholic relations in Ireland, this being a period when Northern Ireland was in deep conflict with protestant England. However, it is just possible that Paignton's first known Rossiter was actually involved in government work, because during his service in Ireland his son Richard became steward for the Blounts of Paignton who were at this time also employed by the government. On their return to Paignton, possibly for their retirement, they brought Richard back with them.

Richard settled in Paignton and in 1745 was married in Paignton's parish church. In 1754 his third son, William, was born in the old Blagdon farmhouse (since demolished) next to Collaton St Mary Church and it is from him two of the best-known local Rossiter families have descended. Thanks to the late Revd Mr Lyde-Hunt's diary we know quite a lot about one of William's ten children. His name was Samuel and he was born in 1793. He apparently grew into an immensely fat man, so big that he used an artificial support, said to be a wheelbarrow, for his stomach, and he also travelled around in a white gig. Mr Lyde-Hunt also stated that 'John Rossiter (b. 1758) the fourth son of Richard, and William's younger brother, continued living in the same house, but rented the farm from some relatives in America', which rather suggests the American relatives perhaps descended from a sibling of that first Rossiter in Paignton in 1684, who perhaps let out the farm to another member of the family before emigrating. Whatever, as time went on John's payments were ignored so he stopped sending money and eventually the farm became his.

Interestingly it is recorded that William's eldest son Richard (b. 1779) went abroad in about 1801; further it is also recorded there was once a Rossiter who became a magistrate and was responsible for deporting a member of the family to Australia! Certainly it is known there had been a rift in the family somewhere in the past and a lot of Rossiters did emigrate to Australia and New Zealand.

Then came the long awaited Emancipation Act of 1829, which gave Catholic families the freedom to partake fully in public life and hold offices under the crown; presumably this is when those Rossiters who hung onto the Catholic faith were able legally to run a business such as their mill at Shorton.

These milling Rossiters went on to own a considerable amount of property around Paignton and it was one of Richard's great grandsons, another John, who moved down into Paignton after his mill in Shorton was burned down in 1835 and leased Paignton's old thatched watermill from Finney Belfield (lord of the manor). In 1837 John accepted the office of first registrar in Paignton. Paignton's old mill, then known as Town Mills in Mill Road (now Mill Lane), was where he almost certainly installed the latest technology of steam power complete with typical tall chimney. The family operated this mill for forty-three years until his son, William Henry, succeeded him and with his great-uncle John Reap, entered into a partnership that continued until the council took over the water rights. It is said that the family continued living in the Mill House, but the 1881 census shows a William Henry Rossiter was resident in Fernham Nursery, Preston. The conservatory in the photograph below is where William Henry sold his produce. William Henry's son

Fernham Nursery, today a shop on Torquay Road. (*D. Caine*)

Harry Bernard Rossiter, who had up to this time not been involved in the milling business, having had a corn merchant's business of his own, possibly the shop in Winner Street, was drawn into it when he formed the Torbay Mill Co., to take over his business in 1900, which stood where the Palace Theatre is now.

Harry Bernard, now a director and no longer involved in his own business, was free to enter into other enterprises; and one in particular was with Isaac Singer's personal engineer, designing the Marist Brother's chapel on St Mary's Hill. The Marist Fathers, having arrived in Paignton a few years before, were the first Catholic order in Paignton for 300 years. However, Henry B's section of the Rossiter family, having remained faithful to the old religion, and because of Henry's involvement with the Seminary chapel, were invited to worship there until 1898 when the Marist Fathers converted the Baptist chapel in Colley End. Before this Henry B's father, William Henry, used to take the local faithful in his personal coach and four to either Lord Clifford's chapel in Chudleigh or nearby Torre Abbey.

The Winner Street mill remained in operation until 1886 when excavations for the Public Hall – later the Palace Theatre – started and the mill business was moved to a more modern establishment next to the station, which is not surprising seeing old William Henry was guarantor of the GWR, Paignton area. His son, Henry B, eventually became vice-chairman of the Torquay and Paignton

H.B. Rossiter and Robert Waycott. (*Peggy Parnell*)

Gas Co., and by 1890 was also extremely interested in the town's controversial project, the new Public Hall-cum-Theatre and was deeply involved in its first production of Gilbert & Sullivan's *Pirates of Penzance*, leading eventually to the formation of the Paignton Operatic and Dramatic Society.

Harry Bernard's half brother, another William, is thought to have had several sons, including one named Paul who carried on the milling business following his father's death up until shortly after the Second World War when the mill was nationalised and he realised he no longer had an inheritance. Broken-hearted he died soon after.

Whatever the relationships between the various Rossiter families, in 1936 Mr (Willo) William Rossiter of Clifton Road, having acted as a deputy to his father William Charles, inherited the office of local Registrar of Births, Deaths and Marriages, and to confirm his family lineage, his daughter told a school friend that her great-grandfather was a miller/farmer in Collaton St Mary. Over the course of 113 years there wasn't a baby born, or a couple married, that a member of the Rossiter family didn't know about. But in 1953 the last in a long line of registrars, William (Willo) Rossiter, retired and to this day is still remembered by many a Paigntonian.

Apart from being registrars, it was the milling business that this Rossiter family were mainly involved in. But all good things come to an end and sadly John Rossiter's old steam mill in Mill Lane, off Littlegate Road, was finally demolished and in its place arose St John's Court, warden-protected flats for the elderly, and so ended 300 years of milling in this area of Paignton.

The enumerator arrived home in the middle of his busiest period of the 1951 census, to find his wife had gone to hospital to have their baby, which was not expected for another week.

Commented Mr Rossiter, 'That baby's smart, he wanted to be in the census.'

Herald Express

THE SHOPKEEPERS' TALE

According to Robinson's 1851 Directory of Paignton, John Rossiter was the owner of a corn, seed merchant and nursery shop in Winner Street, he was also a Registrar of Births, Deaths and Marriages. In due course his son, George, acquired the shop at the junction of Winner Street with Church Street, called Eastleigh House, one of a cluster of three separate properties – one of which he opened up as a gun dealer, articles and second-hand shop. Eventually he too inherited the office of Registrar. This house, together with the two other properties attached, actually formed an island and George's home was the two-storeyed building with windows facing onto Church Street. Facing onto the Winner Street side was another shop which it is thought also belonged to him. Sandwiched between these two houses was a tiny cottage of two rooms with an equally minute garden complete with iron railings. Because these three houses formed an island, George Rossiter was nicknamed 'Robinson Crusoe'. In the early 1900s George's shop on the Church Street side changed hands and a Miss Evans, together with her father, a

Rossiter's corn and seed shop in Winner Street. (*Frank Pearce*, Torbay The Golden Years, *Halsgrove, 2002*)

George Rossiter's shop in Church Street. (*Frank Pearce*, Torbay The Golden Years, *Halsgrove, 2002*)

The Narrows, Winner Street, *c.* 1950, painted by Frank Chubb. (*Peggy Parnell*)

tailor, opened it as a drapery shop. Eventually she inherited the business and became well known in Paignton. Unfortunately during the 1960s this unique triangle of buildings was demolished, but not before a painting was done of the narrows behind by local artist Frank Chubb.

DESCRIPTIVE CATALOGUE

OF

FRUIT TREES

Ornamental, Evergreen and Deciduous Shrubs

CONIFERÆ, ROSES, CLIMBERS, &c.

CULTIVATED FOR SALE BY

WM. CHARLES ROSSITER

Nurseryman and Seed Merchant

11 Victoria Street

PAIGNTON

All communications to be addressed to VICTORIA STREET, Paignton.

One of William Charles Rossiter's adverts. (*D. Caine*)

Henry Bernard and William (Willo) Rossiter were cousins and Willo's father, William Charles Rossiter, whom it is presumed took on the office of Registrar from George, also owned a garden shop in Victoria Street as well as a furniture shop in Winner Street, where as a boy Willo was apprenticed to Mr Lidstone the ironmonger. When Henry Bernard formed the new Torbay Mill company it is presumed it was he who opened a shop facing onto Winner Street where a young lad named Gerry Rundle was employed, a rotund chap who, with his ready smile and a cheery word for all, became one of the most popular personalities in Paignton.

It is known the first family of Rossiters in Rochester were prolific producers of offspring, the descendants of which have spread far and wide, all following various occupations. In Paignton William H, although now retired, was still true to his corn milling and agricultural origins, and with his ancestor's astuteness for business continued supplying produce to the many businesses around the area until he died. One of these businesses was his nursery in Fernham near Oldway. A glass conservatory acted as his shop where people came and bought his freshly picked produce, and if a patron happened to be a tenant she or he could call into his smallholding next door to pay their rent. In one of his houses was a chap who kept pigs and a young Michael Adams remembered being taken regularly to see a sow with her never-ending production of piglets!

In 1858 two of Richard's great-granddaughters, rather surprisingly to the then widely spread agricultural community, opened a small double-fronted building

The Misses Rossiter's first shop, 1858. (*Lilian Hobbs*)

towards the west end of Winner Street. At the time Miss Sara and Miss Jane Rossiter's venture was considered foolhardy, for Paignton had few visitors, mainly gentry, who took up residence for the summer months only. Perhaps the girls realised these visiting ladies had a need, for in that year a new style of dress became the rage: 'the crinoline' was in and the 'hoop skirt' out. This dramatic new style was what every fashion-conscious woman wanted, from maidservant to lady. So the Misses Rossiter did know what they were doing and they never looked back. The business continued to grow and Sarah remained involved until her death in 1923.

An extract from *The Court Journal* dated 5 October 1911 explains the high standard that Sarah and her family attained:

> To Miss Rossiter was given the honour of producing the magnificent
> Coronation gown worn by Her Majesty The Queen on June 22nd 1911,
> as well as a large number of elegant toilettes designed and made for
> various functions, including the Queen's forthcoming visit to India.

Sarah married a tea clipper captain and mercer also called Rossiter, and in 1888 their son Frank became enthusiastically involved in the business. It was he who decided to move their shop into one of the new business units in Palace Avenue, which has remained in the family ever since.

CHAPTER SEVEN

Stories from the Old Town

ONE GREEN BOTTLE

In 1979 a local newspaper reported the story of a 200-year-old bottle seal found by Mr James Houlton of 24 Grange Road, Paignton, which he discovered embedded in his garden wall. The bottle was made of dark green glass, a type made in the eighteenth century for the gentry who sealed their bottles before returning them to the brewery for re-filling. The merchant's imprint on this bottle was, 'F. Millman, Paignton, 1776'.

Research into the Millman name revealed the family to be related by marriage to the Goodridges who owned brew-houses and malt-houses around the area during the eighteenth century. In October 1759, at the age of twenty-four, Francis Millman married Susanna Vicary at Sandford and their grandson, Daniel by name, became the innkeeper of the Oldenburg Inn from 1843 to 1850 under its previous name of The Globe and apparently paid £7 10s per year highway rates. Daniel's father was Thomas Millman and it was his father, Francis Millman, whose name was on the bottle seal.

Between 1692 and 1718 the vicar of Paignton and Marldon was a Revd Francis Millman and in his will, dated 2 July 1718, he mentions his mother and his son, then at Oxford, as well as William Kitson Senior, Lord of the Manor of Shiphay, and Thomas Butland of Paignton, both of whom were well-known names among the gentry of Torbay. Another ancestor was Dean Millman, writer of the hymn 'Ride on, Ride on in Majesty', a popular and stirring hymn among church congregations even to this day. So we may be sure the Millmans moved in the best of circles. The New Pier Inn, situated in Goodrington Road (now Roundham Road) and owned by William Maclean, was completed in 1849 and tenanted out by him. The following year the Pier Inn was opened by his tenant who happened to be the owner of the green bottle – Francis Millman. (Ernest Britton, *The Oldenburg Hotel*, 1990)

CASE OF THE DISSOLVING PILLAR!

Around the corner from Palace Avenue, in Winner Street, is the old hotel and coaching inn known as The Oldenburg, with a fine eighteenth-century porch gracing the oldest part of the road. One day, on looking out from the window of her shop opposite the hotel, the proprietress was watching the constant flow of

The Oldenburg Hotel. (*Peggy Parnell*)

heavy traffic which at this time plied both ways through Winner Street, and was thinking to herself that two-way traffic with such huge lorries was far too much for such a narrow street, when suddenly there was a loud bang. The top of a huge meat wagon caught the corner of the old porch and as the van drove on, the driver totally oblivious, one of the old pillars dissolved in front of her eyes. Sadly, the remaining pillar was removed and with it another piece of Paignton's history.

IN SEARCH OF MUM

During the late 1950s there used to be three lock-up shops (currently Solo Stores) almost directly opposite the entrance to Palace Avenue. The owner of these shops was a small Edwardian gentleman with tousled white hair, who was always attired in a tobacco-spotted jacket, grey waistcoat with silver watch chain and pinstripe trousers. Mr Dark ran a small Umbrella Factory and Fancy Goods business in the largest of his three shops and his workshop at the back was an Aladdin's Cave full of the most amazing things; here he mended many objets d'art as well as making and repairing umbrellas. Over his shop door was written 'By Royal Appointment', to whom or for what is not known, but at a guess he might have supplied and repaired umbrellas for royal visitors. His little shop at the other end of the block, measuring 11ft x 8ft, was for a few years during the

Second World War Paignton's coal office where people exchanged fuel coupons for their allowance of coal, coke or anthracite. In the mid-1950s it was let to an electrical contracting business. Like all the other old cottages along Winner Street the toilet facilities were almost non-existent – in this case one passed through a wooden gate at the side of the shop up a rough path to the rear of the property to a timber shed with no window and a rough wooden seat over a hole. One day the then proprietor's mother came to visit and on requesting the toilet she was directed to this outbuilding. A busy morning ensued and on such occasions the proprietor's mother would often go off shopping. At one o'clock the husband suggested perhaps they should go in search of mum. They did and found the poor soul trapped in that dark, decrepit, spider-infested, primitive space called a 'toilet' with no light and no one to hear her cries for help!

THE BLACKSMITH

In the 1920s the east side of Winner Street still had a number of properties with thatched roofs, although these were gradually being replaced by slate, as much to prevent fire as for modernisation. Several of these old properties in 1808 were,

Paignton's old smithy was like this one at Morwellham Quay, on the River Tamar. (*Peggy Parnell*)

and still are, the remains of old (enclosed) court farms. At the junction of Winner Hill and Winner Street was the town's smithy owned and run by Matthew Pope, a fantastic character whose smithy, now a private dwelling, was blackened by years of smoke, with tools of every imaginable shape hanging on the walls and where little boys viewed in awe the interior with its strange sounds and smells. Here Matthew, equally as black as the walls, could be found most days bending over his anvil, hammering red-hot iron into the shape of a waiting horse's hoof. A great mystery for many a youngster watching the process of this craft was why the horse didn't jolt when the red-hot shoe was fitted to its hoof!

CHAPTER EIGHT

Tribulations of Dairymen

TWO SONS OF A DAIRYMAN

Around 1937/8 it was quite the thing for the young sons of dairymen to help their fathers deliver 10 gallons of milk every day. One particular case involved the two sons of Leo the dairyman in Church Street, grandchildren of Mitchell, a well-known local dairy farmer. Each morning these two young lads would load 10 gallons of milk onto their father's home-made wagon, constructed from a soapbox and fixed to two pram wheels with a handle for guiding it. After school each day

One lad resplendent on his new bike with Head's dairy/grocery shop in the background.
(*D. Head*)

the boys returned home, washed out and refilled all the bottles they had collected and when the job was done they stored the bottles overnight in a huge walk-in refrigerator constructed of concrete blocks. For this work the boys were paid 2s 6d a week as wages. Believe it or not this was good money, for many of their chums only got 1s and some even as little as 6d. Out of this pay the boys were expected to fund all their desires. As good as their pay was it didn't cover the cost of new bikes, so their father advanced them £5 each on the promise of a weekly repayment.

It so happened a new law had just been passed to stop young lads under fourteen years of age being given the heavy job of delivering milk before eight in the morning. Father was disgusted for he knew no wages meant no repayments and the boys had already taken delivery of their new bikes, so neither Father nor the lads took any notice of the new law and continued their milk rounds. About this time a new school inspector, a man with one arm, was employed to supervise such youngsters. The inspector was specifically told to keep an eye on this particular family. Knowing full well what he was up against, he made regular visits to the Church Street dairy in order to persuade the mother to stop her lads doing early morning milk rounds, but to no avail. In fact it became a real cat-and-mouse game with mum repeatedly fobbing 'Mr B' off and Father regularly ducking the issue. Then one day Father spotted the inspector coming down the street and, quickly hiding behind a door, listened to everything that was said. When the inspector finished, Father, with steam issuing from his ears, rushed out to tell him in no uncertain terms that it was a good job he only had one arm! That did it for good and all. Father was beaten maybe, but not bowed; he still found jobs for the boys to do so they never finished before six o'clock of an evening, on top of which they had to be home by eight o'clock sharp. So the lads would spend their free time cycling around town until one minute to eight when they returned home and, sitting on their bikes outside their back gate, watched the parish church clock until it struck the hour before entering the house!

It was because of cases such as this that the age limit was introduced, the education authority considering young boys would not have enough energy to carry out such heavy work and attend school as well. They were quite wrong. These two lads, thin as they were, had no problems, for after completing their morning deliveries they would be off on their bikes, probably to get away from any further work their father could find them, arriving in school long before nine o'clock with more than enough energy for a day's work. Father never failed to have a dig at the poor inspector whenever the chance arose. He always ended up promising to comply, but of course never did!

DAD'S STORY

Dad may well have been ill educated, but he was no fool. Sadly he was made to leave school at eleven years of age, for it was thought they could teach him no more. It's just possible he was seriously dyslexic, but in those days this was not understood. However, Leo made up for his losses in educational abilities by being a strong, well-built young man, capable at the age of twelve of using a plough with two 'orses, as he would say. It so happened that his father had a contract with the local authority to supply horses and carts for haulage between various public works. Leo often worked with him and one day the council foreman, for a laugh, sent young Leo up to the council yard for a 'long weight', but Leo was no fool and turned the trick to his advantage by spending two hours out of the way and entering it on his timesheet. On passing the sheet in, the foreman hastily remarked, 'T'em I'll not pay for that, t'were only a joke.'

'But,' replied Leo, 't'were only what foreman asked me to do!'

He got his money and the foreman got a strong lesson that Leo was no ignoramus!

GRANDDAD'S STORY

Before electrically operated ice-cream makers came into use, Leo's father, Mitchell, puffing away on his pipe with curtains drawn to keep out the sun, turned the ice-cream bowl by hand, occasionally adding broken pieces of ice to keep the temperature down. Towards the end of the process he would sometimes get his two young grandsons to finish off the job. The lads soon learnt two minutes longer increased the volume and considered they could safely help themselves to a taster, but Grandfather always knew!

Between the two world wars it was common practice for local dairy farmers to buy and sell livestock in Totnes market once a week, and Grandfather Mitchell was one of them. When the morning's dealings and the greater part of business was over, most of the farmers would retire to the nearest pub, Grandfather with them, spending the rest of the day sampling various local brews of cider. By the end of the proceedings so drunk was Grandfather that his less inebriated chums would heave him onto his trap and with a slap on the pony's rump send the obedient animal trotting over the bridge, through Bridgetown in the direction of home and stable. On arrival the old boy, still unconscious, was lifted off his cart and put safely to bed, his faithful pony returned to his stable to collect his reward.

Bill Maunder was an excellent gardener who worked a piece of land behind the herbalist shop on the corner of Church Street and Well Street. His garden was reached via a steep flight of steps behind the shop. Bill and his wife were devoted to one another and as a dutiful wife she always made sure he went to work in a clean white apron. Following her death, however, he went to pieces. He kept his garden going but went to live with his sister at the other end of Well Street, and no matter how hard she tried Bill would never wear clean clothes. He eventually became an unkempt recluse living in his garden shed. During the Second World War Bill, being a man of few words, took to getting his meagre rations from Leo's dairy, 2oz of butter and 4oz of margarine, insisting on calling the latter 'cart grease'. It was on his visits to the shop that he struck up a friendship with Grandfather Mitchell. When the old boy died Bill obviously missed him very much, for on the day of his funeral he entered the shop carrying a gigantic bouquet of beautiful flowers which he awkwardly thrust into the daughter-in-law's arms, saying in broad Devonian, 'Yer be some flowers. Put 'em at Mitchell's veet.'

A Daw's Creamery milk
churn used until well after
the Second World War.
(*Peggy Parnell*)

KEEP THEM ROLLING

In the far-off days of dairy farmers, that is before the Second World War, to
have a van for very large deliveries was quite up-market, but one with a door
that stayed shut would have been sheer luxury for one particular dairyman who
one day, when driving up the steep end of Blatchcombe Road, his van loaded
to capacity with several large milk churns filled to the brim, suddenly heard an
almighty bang and with a quick look in his mirror, saw to his horror all his churns
rolling downhill in a river of milk!

CHAPTER NINE

A Prince Calls

Although the story of William of Orange and his landing in Brixham is well known, research into various records and early books has helped to dispel the myth that Paignton had no involvement in these events. In fact it was not only Brixham and Paignton but also much of the countryside around that felt the full brunt of William's massive invasion force on 5 November 1688 and the two days following his bloodless invasion as it slowly moved across this corner of Devon.

On 19 October 1688 Prince William of Orange sailed his flotilla of Dutch ships northwards into a severe gale so bad that he was forced to turn the fleet back into his port of Hellevoetsluis, where they threw overboard hundreds of horses killed in the storm. Undaunted, Prince William had his fleet repaired and on 1 November made again for the North Sea. But still the weather was against him so he abandoned his plans for Hull and, taking advantage of the wind, manoeuvred his fleet of 300 ships carrying 15,000 men, 3,000 horses and 200 cannon, together with a backup force of sixty-five warships, down the channel past Dover and Portsmouth, moving steadily towards Torbay. It is just possible William might have been aiming for the port of Dartmouth or even Plymouth, but by 4 November in severe weather conditions he was fast approaching Torbay, a bay well known to the Dutch sailors for its deep draft, so with gale-force winds blowing he probably reasoned the bay could offer the fleet some protection. By the time the fleet arrived it was too dark for landing. In fact the weather was so harsh the fleet overshot the bay and, although it has been mooted they made an attempt to enter Dartmouth, they eventually turned around and tacked back towards Torbay. After the storms of the past few days it was as if by divine providence that in the early hours of the next morning, 5 November 1688, the wind changed, the rain stopped and the sun rose over a sea that was like a mill-pond with a slight mist hanging over it, dispersing as the sun gained in strength and giving way to a lovely day. Although it is said some troops had landed earlier and were already camping in Paignton, at whatever time the fleet entered Torbay it must have been a fantastic sight for those overlooking the bay to suddenly see on the horizon a huge mass of tall ships approaching in full sail, all flying the Prince of Orange's standard with a white flag uppermost to signify their peaceful intent and a red flag below to represent war to those who disapproved of the Prince's good intentions. As the fleet filled the bay it resembled a city of spires and in no time at all little boats like bees were swarming between the ships, each one decked overall with its colours, a sight likely never seen before in Torbay. Fortunately, thanks to the diaries of Prince William's ministers (clerics), Mr Whittle and Dr Burnett, we are able to peep into some of the extraordinary events that happened over the next two days. But one thing is a certainty – Prince William could never have visualised the difficulties he was about to face while disembarking such a huge force into such a small hamlet as Brixham.

Unaware that King James' army was held up, the Prince immediately set his warships patrolling Lyme Bay. Meanwhile, the level of support in Brixham being unknown, a small flotilla of English Scots Guards (amazing as it may seem, they were resident in Holland) was sent in to learn the strength of feeling for the Prince. According to local historian Charles Gregory, who assured his readers of his care in relating both oral and written testimonies, the officers were more than satisfied with their findings, so they quickly arranged the transfer of the Prince from his ship, the *Harleian Miscellany*, to a smaller vessel, the *Princess Mary*, which sailed into the inlet escorted by four men-o'-war, with local merchant ships and all manner of craft following as close as they dare.

Once the people of Torbay realised it was the Prince of Orange, they ran from their cottages, flocking to the water's edge, along lanes and on top of headlands, indeed anywhere where they could get a good view. At first many thought it might be the French fleet, but on seeing the Prince's standard a great cheer went up and as the ships sailed close into Brixham the locals were able to follow them along the pathways. Suddenly a loud bang pierced the air; for a moment the world must have stopped, but it was only the Admiral of Rotterdam who had given orders for guns to be fired as he drew alongside the quay!

The ships carrying Prince William's lords, nobles, gentlemen and officers eventually drew alongside so close that they could see the local people and in turn the Brixham people could hear them talking on the ships. One of the Prince's ministers went to the uppermost cabin of the ship *Golden Sun*, and pulling a Bible from his pocket, flourished it aloft in his right hand so that the citizens could see their intentions, at the same time shouting, 'It is the Prince of Orange that comes!' In anticipation of relief from the tyranny of King James II, the people were delighted and shouted for joy. As the Prince's vessel drew nearer, at about one o'clock in the afternoon on 5 November he was transferred into a small barge and rowed towards the quay where the oarsmen endeavoured to pull alongside a short pier, but the barge stuck fast. It is thought this landing stage was sited nearby an ancient quay built into shallow water in about 1300 and this could well have been why the royal barge grounded. However, the inhabitants of Brixham had already come down to the beach in large numbers to greet Prince William, but before attempting to land the Prince stood up in his barge and spoke to the people in broken English: 'Mine goot people, mine goot people, I mean you goot; I am here for your goot, for all your goots.' Fortunately the people understood what he meant and a Brixham man named Youlden replied on their behalf, 'You'm welcome'.

The Prince responded, 'If I am welcome, then come and carry me ashore.' Immediately, so the legend goes, a burly fisherman named Peter Varwell dashed into the sea and with guardsmen on all sides carried on his shoulders the slightly built frame of the future King of England. As the Prince of Orange stepped ashore his standard was unfurled and that respected citizen Mr Youlden came forward to deliver a welcoming speech, which according to legend and in the fashion of the day was in doggerel rhyme. Some 200 years later a potter in Aller Vale, Torquay, threw a commemorative mug inscribed with the very words addressed to His Majesty on that day in 1688:

'And it please your Majesty King William,
You'm welcome to Brixham Quay,
To eat 'Buckhorn'* and drink 'Bohea'** along o' we.

This poem was the first time that the prince was referred to as king.

Over the centuries the Dutch archives have adamantly opposed the Peter Varwell story, saying it was nothing more than local folklore and refusing to accept that an ordinary fisherman would have been allowed to get anywhere near the prince. They say William was a very distrusting man and could be a dangerous person to deal with. He apparently had his own secret service and was heavily protected by his personal guards. They say that when the Royal Barge grounded short of the old harbour he was much more likely to have been carried ashore by one of his personal officers. But maybe William was more astute than they realised and saw this as a good public relations act. Neither do the Dutch specify how the Prince actually got onto dry land or where he spent his first night, but they do say the man who carried the Prince ashore was later given the captaincy of a ship, but was he rewarded for physically carrying the Prince ashore or for ferrying him close to the shoreline where Varwell carried him to the beach? In any event, neither Prince William nor his men had any need to worry, for the whole of Brixham and all the settlements around welcomed him with open arms and heartily cheered when his standard, bearing the words *Libertate Et Religion Je Maintiendray* (Liberty and Religion I Will Uphold), was unfurled.

Fortunately the diaries of William's ministers together with various local writings all substantiate what the Brixham people have said, in particular the Varwell story. Varwell's descendants, have also strongly upheld the accuracy of the story and according to one descendant of the family, a Miss Varwell who was a valued and well-known Brixham schoolteacher in the 1930s and friend of a well-respected Brixham family, maintained to her dying day that it was her ancestor who waded out to the barge and carried the prince ashore on his back. There is also a nice local story told by an elderly fisherman that Varwell apparently detailed his six-year-old son to keep vigil during the night with a lit candle in the window of his father's attic, just in case the Prince and his lords managed to get

---

*   Buckhorn is the fish whiting, split down through the back then salted and dried.
**   Bohea – a kind of tea.

ashore in the dark. Interestingly Varwell's house, where the Prince is reputed to have stayed, certainly had a high attic window.

There were many stories told about this momentous time. One in particular was that of a man named Samuel Wyndeatt, who on hearing the news grabbed his eight-year-old son, mounted his horse, placing his little lad in front of him, and galloped at great speed from Totnes just for a glimpse of the Prince. Another tale is of a supporter, also from Totnes, who on hearing the news from his grandchildren in Paignton sent a wagonload of apples. Another well-wisher from Staverton brought a cartload of apples to the crossroads outside Paignton, shouting to the passing soldiers to help themselves. Apples were, of course, plentiful at this time of the year. One young lady walked to Brixham, boldly shook hands with the prince and was promptly given a handful of proclamations to hand out – and forgot to keep one for herself. Generally people from far and wide brought Prince William's men all manner of provisions and tokens, for which William's men were truly grateful and amply repaid the donors.

Prince William's personal chaplain, the Revd Dr Burnet, wrote in his diary that once on shore the prince with Marshal Schomberg and others set about obtaining as many horses as the locals could spare. On these horses the Prince and his lords, knights and gents, with trumpets sounding, 'hautboyes' playing, drums beating and his colours flying before him, marched up Overgang onto Furzeham Hill, where people ran out of their cottages to see the sight and cheer. Even the fleet below could see and hear the huzzahs and responded with loud cheers. All this happened many times during their stay.

On Furzeham Common with its uninterrupted view of the bay and beyond, the Prince set up camp for his soldiers, choosing a good position where his men could stand at arms throughout the night should James' army attack. Today it seems strange that he didn't use Berry Head, but of course the settlement was then on the other side of a long inlet. As soon as Prince William had his troops organised he sent a pre-arranged message, would you believe in the form of a quince, to the Earl of Bath at Plymouth to inform him that his army had landed in England, and according to William's Revd Mr Whittle he then spent his first day and night on English soil in Middle Street, Brixham, taking over Varwell's house as his administration office. Here, in the heart of Brixham, is where he received his first dignitary, Nicholas Roope from Dartmouth, followed by many other landowners from around the area. However, it is also reputed that the Prince slept in Hill House, although there is no documentation to prove this, what documents there are show that part of this property has ancient origins and passed through the hands of a long line of nobles such as the Pomeroy-Gilberts, the Champernownes and Henry Grey, father of the tragic Lady Jane Grey, beheaded by Mary I. Following this unfortunate incident the property became Crown land, but it is very likely that the dwelling would still have been held by a gentleman of some note. Whichever house Prince William spent the night in, all his Dutch lords, noblemen, officers and gentlemen were quartered around him with a section of his Horse Guards and some of the infantry protecting them. A particularly strong guard was set up outside where the prince slept. It is possible that Hill House is where the Prince received local dignitaries.

The section of Hill House to the left of the picture is the oldest part, dating from 1206.
(*Peggy Parnell*)

One has to realise that at the time of William's arrival Lower Brixham consisted of little more than a few hamlets. As one can imagine it was packed to capacity with hundreds of officers who crammed to suffocation into the only alehouse, where it is reputed the barman strutted like a peacock as he was serving so many lords and nobles!

By coincidence, 5 November was the anniversary of the Gunpowder Plot, ever since known in Brixham as 'No Popery Night'. The Prince received many well-wishers who were Protestant Nonconformists and particularly those from Totnes, who were thankful to be able to return to Parliament their recorder Sir Edward Seymour, instead of the Catholic Sir John Southcote of Dartmouth. Here the Prince also received Sir William Courtenay's son who invited him to use Ford House, his home in Newton Abbot.

King William's Cottage. (*Peggy Parnell*)

Prince William's huge army, consisting of 26 regiments, 15,400 men, about 1,000 officers and 78 field officers, disembarked all that day and the following night onto Furzeham Common and the surrounding areas, totally unaware of the conditions they were about to encounter. The troops who apparently landed earlier had camped on the outskirts of Paignton and were recovering from a terrible night; for although it had been clear and frosty, the ground was wet and soggy from recent heavy rains. Indeed the whole force, discovering the terrible conditions, quickly made bonfires by cutting down hedges, using green wood, farm gates, old doors or indeed anything that would burn. Apparently a private in search of a convenient spot happened upon an enclosure full of turnips and carried as many as he could to his fire. Very soon all were boiling or roasting turnips with their pieces of Dutch beef, although a few ate the turnips raw. Others managed to find chickens. Some soldiers went into nearby villages and bought a few provisions, particularly for their officers who, having been at sea so long, were eager to obtain certain refreshments! Alas there was little to be found. Nevertheless all had a good meal that night washed down with their own Dutch ale. Several hundred fires were lit on Furzeham alone, so few people could have missed the activities.

After satisfying their hunger the men on Furzeham Common, who were not standing to arms, sought out their sheltered resting places and, protected by their heavy army coats and boots, dug in for the night. To stay warm and dry was a problem, so wet and squelchy was the ground that in the morning many found themselves covered in the sticky red mud of Devon, for that night it rained heavily again and those who lost their way in the country lanes fared the worst, for there were no guides to advise them and in the dark no visible means of shelter; with rain entering every part of their clothing it must have been sheer hell! The next day was no better, with carts and heavy gear getting stuck in ruts of deep red mud. For all this the troops were well disciplined, even though the rough seas they had recently endured left them with the feeling that the ground was heaving. They were glad not to have been called to arms as they would have been worse than useless.

The Prince's immediate problem was how to get the large number of horses ashore, so he called on all the Brixham fishermen to advise how and where they could do this. The cautious Brixham men pondered the problem, saying it would take days to move such a huge cargo! However, in 1688 the deep inlet reached up to Bolton Cross and here, where the Baptist church now stands, the officers were advised they would be able to offload their lighter equipment at high tide, but were recommended to send their heavy equipment, armoury, carts, goods and money wagons by sea to Topsham, near Exeter. But 4,000 horses – that was different! The fishermen then took the officers to a place nearby Comber's Bottom (near Cumber's Hill) and here they successfully disembarked the animals. One fisherman who helped land some of the horses recalled how these were put overboard to swim the short distance ashore with only a single rope from ship to shore to guide them. Another witnessed a shipload of horses come right up to the quayside and walk off already harnessed, and this fisherman was even more surprised at the speed each man found and mounted his horse. To the amazement of the fishermen all 4,000 horses were safely landed by morning.

Meanwhile boats kept coming in packed with officers and soldiers, all instructed to disembark at great speed lest King James' army descend upon them. However, they were more likely to lose their lives scrambling out of the boats with their heavy gear; some landed in shallow water while others were up to their ears in water and nearly drowned. In their haste many an oar was broken.

According to a letter dated 1 December 1688, one of the first things Prince William did was to command one of his worthy captains to search all Catholic houses in the area such as Ugbrook, Chudleigh and Lady Cary's house at Torre Abbey for arms and horses. Lady Carey entertained the soldiers civilly, explaining that her husband was away in Plymouth. The men collected some horses and a few arms and troubled the household no further. However, while there they learnt that a priest staying in the abbey, while looking out to sea, saw the fleet approaching and on seeing white flags concluded it must be the French fleet they had so long expected. Overjoyed he ordered all to sing the *Te Deum* as the 'French' entered the Abbey. In anticipation of this great event the monks had stored considerable provisions for a welcoming feast, but instead of 'Vostre serviteur Monsieur' the

Torre Abbey as it was at the time of William's arrival. (*From Deryck Seymour's* Torre Abbey, *1977*)

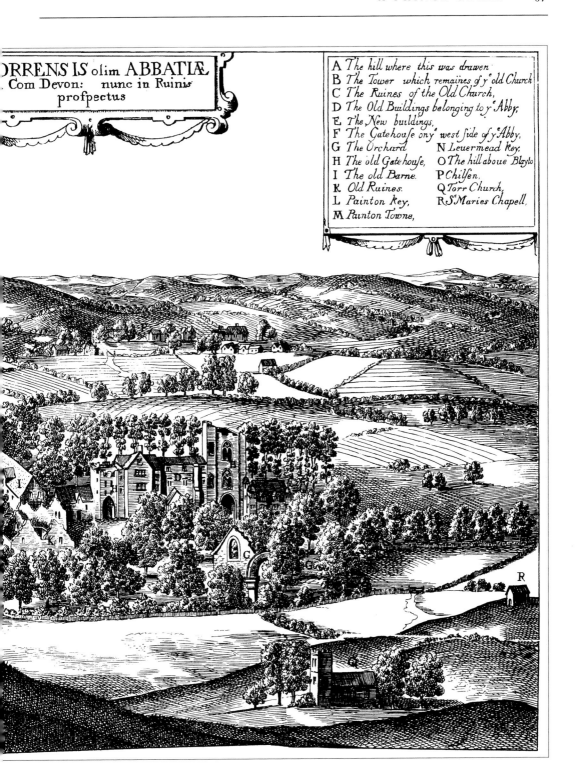

ORRENS IS olim ABBATIÆ
Com Devon: nunc in Ruinis
prospectus

A *The hill where this was drawen*
B *The Tower which remaines of y'e old Church*
C *The Ruines of the Old Church,*
D *The Old Buildings belonging to y'e Abby,*
E *The New buildings,*
F *The Gatehouse ony'e west side of y'e Abby,*
G *The Orchard*   N *Leuermead key,*
H *The old Gatehouse,* O *The hill aboue Blayto*
I *The old Barne.*   P *Chilsen,*
K *Old Ruines.*   Q *Torr Church,*
L *Painton key,*   R *S'e Maries Chapell,*
M *Painton Towne,*

Abbey inmates were greeted with 'Yeen Mynheer – can you Dutch spraken?' Upon which the whole household fled, excepting Lady Cary and several old and faithful servants – and the Dutchmen soon put those hoarded provisions to good use! Stories that the Dutch burnt down the abbey before leaving were just malicious talk; in fact some officers and men actually stayed in the house.

On the following morning, 6 November, Prince William with some of his nobles reviewed the troops on Furzeham Common, but later a mystery unfolded as to the Prince's whereabouts, for Constantine Huygens, the Prince's personal secretary who was normally to be found at his side, was apparently much concerned about where his master had gone. According to the Dutch Royal Household archives, Huygens wrote in his diary, 'on the day after landing, the Prince left with the infantry and he himself left Brixham a short time after marching the army through Churston, Goodrington, Wynerde St (Winner Street) and Fore Street (Church Street)'.

This march is clearly portrayed in a contemporary Dutch drawing showing the route taken, but on Huygens' arrival in Paignton it was dark and he could not find the Prince's quarters; he was obviously concerned to establish that he had arrived.

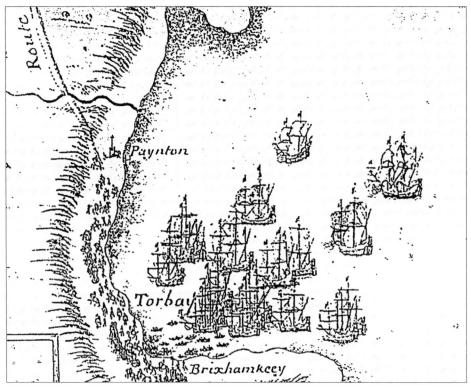

The Dutch marching to Paignton, possibly sketched by one of Prince William's officers or his minister. (*Ernest Britton, PP&LHS*)

Eventually he was told they were at King's Castel (Huygens spelling). The march into Paignton was later substantiated by an undated letter written in French in about 1697 and found among the Earl of Denbigh's commissioned report on his manuscripts. It read, 'on the sixth we marched to Paignton, a village situated on the other side of the bay'.

One can but wonder at the vision those Dutch soldiers had of old Paignton on that cold damp November day in 1688 as they approached the ruins of the old Bishop's Palace with its crenulated walls and reputed twin towers. What they possibly saw as they approached were the church tower and nearby Bishops Tower. But who knows, they could just be right for it is understood that a second tower once existed. Studies now show that there were towers on many manorial sites in the late Anglo-Saxon period, about 1000 AD. Is it possible that this was the ruin of one still in existence in 1688?

For many years it was considered pure folklore that William of Orange stayed in Paignton, although one would think the Prince, while passing through, must have at least addressed the good citizens of Paignton. For a long time it was thought Paigntonians got his declaration confused with the one that that took place in Newton Abbot the next day, when Prince William's minister, Revd John Whittle, stood on what was probably a 'Brutus' stone and read a lengthy declaration issued by the Prince of Orange at a place called 'Cross' near St Leonard's Tower. Interestingly the inscription on this stone was later found to be incorrect.

New information about a stone in front of the west door of Paignton's parish church, for years considered to be from an old font, has recently come to hand which gives a different explanation of its history. Firstly, a comment in a guidebook by D.H. Higgs in about 1900 refers to an old cross: 'this cross stood almost in the centre of the higher part of Church Street and from the steps of an ancient worked cross, William Prince of Orange was proclaimed to the people of Paignton.'

Secondly, this record ties in nicely with the Revd Mr Lyde-Hunt's journal in the Devon Records Office, in which he states:

> The base of the 'Market Cross' now at the west end of the church was given to the church by the late Dr Pridham[*], the trustee of the late H. Kellock Esq.: it had been removed from 'The Croft' which was once the grange of the Precentor (now incorporated in the site of the hospital). It had been taken there by the Nash[**] family, who hollowed the stone out and used it as a pig trough. Its original position was at Highcross (now part of Church Street). The octagonal platform and cross in the middle of the road was destroyed in 1871 by the 'Local Board' in digging for a sewer.

---

[*]   Penwill, in his book *Paignton in Six Reigns*, states that in 1865 Dr Pridham was deeply involved with the sewerage problems of the town.
[**] No record of the Nash family has been found.

This lithograph shows the shaft of Paignton's market/preacher's cross which it is said was damaged by the local children. The present cross was erected in 1895 by an unknown subscription. (*Peggy Parnell*)

The shaft of this market/preacher's cross, typical of many across Devon and Cornwall, was later set up in the churchyard where an old menhir (standing stone) once stood; the base step on which this shaft now rests is said to date from around the thirteenth century.

Interestingly, Paignton's worked cross, one of many such in Devon and Cornwall, would have been similar to the piece of a four-sided lantern-cross found in the grounds of Churston Church which can presently be seen above the Parvise window. It is alleged this type of cross was known locally as a 'Calvary' and it is thought a misspelling of this, in the Pembroke Report on Paignton, gave rise to the area being called 'Culverhay', but much more likely culvery, meaning a pigeon/dovecote, which is known to have existed in Church Street in the mid-sixteenth century.

Taking into consideration the confusion relating to this cross and the historical records, it seems possible that the traditional reading of the Declaration at Paignton's Cross could quite well have became confused with the reading at the Newton Abbot Brutus Stone, and in the course of time only the Newton Abbot reading was remembered.

The remains of a preacher's cross can be seen above the South porch of Churston Church. (*Peggy Parnell*)

Huygens and William were eventually reunited, for there is no doubt that the Prince spent his second night in Devon in the old Posting House, Fore Street (Church Street), Paignton, where apparently for many years the bed he slept in was preserved by the locals. Later, following William's coronation in 1689, the hostelry was renamed with much pride the Crown & Sceptre and later still the Crown & Anchor. This first name has long been considered highly contentious, but it is rather strange that this coaching inn should have been renamed Crown & Sceptre, rather than the Prince William, a name used by so many pubs following his arrival in England. If there was no real connection with the prince and the renaming of this coaching inn, why did Paigntonians, long after this event, still call the building 'King's Castle', as depicted in a lithograph by R. Gale from a sketch by Lady Georgina Northe in 1825? Even this was thought to have

The Crown & Anchor Inn, where Prince William stayed. (*T. Moss*)

Paignton, from a sketch by Georgina Northe. (*Ernest Britton, PP&LHS*)

portrayed a rather liberal degree of artistic licence until Paignton's renowned town surveyor, Frank Penwill (1950s), when asked his opinion, guaranteed that it was a completely accurate interpretation and furthermore that all known deeds and documents upheld everything written relating to these events.

But the mystery still remains: why did the Prince go off on his second day in Devon, taking with him the infantry and no doubt resplendent on his horse with standard flying, his lords and nobles at the rear and his personal guards close at heel, probably with fifes playing and drums beating. Where did he go and for what reason? Well, it is possible he was invited to visit a gentleman of high rank known to reside in the nearby settlement of Yalberton Tor, within the manor of Paignton. So this small army, in three lines with Peter Varwell leading, set off through the lanes towards Churston, onto the high road and across the ridge (the old Brixham Road) to eventually arrive at this nobleman's house in Yalberton. Later the Prince and his guards were guided from there to a large farmhouse at Longcombe, where he was introduced to the men of the west who were among those responsible for encouraging him to come to England, in particular Edward Seymour of Berry Pomeroy, one of the foremost Tory gentlemen of England.

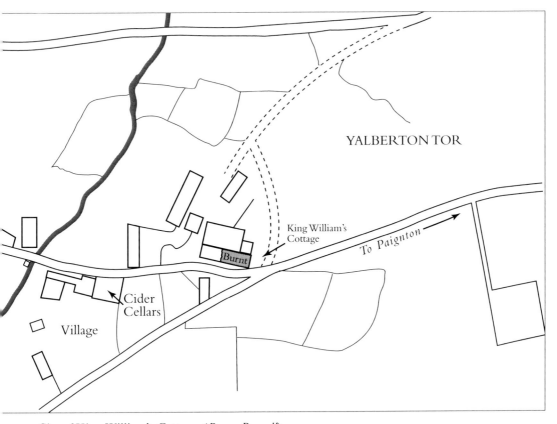

Site of King William's Cottage. (*Peggy Parnell*)

Berry Pomeroy Castle as seen from Afton Woods. (*Peggy Parnell*)

Possibly owing to a mistranslation in the minister's diary, for a long time it was considered that William of Orange spent his second night in the house of this Yalberton nobleman, who it is thought might have been William Courtenay, who shortly after this was made Earl of Devon. At the same time Prince William probably met the Sheriff of Devon who was possibly a descendant by marriage of the Kirkham family and who might have been the Earl of Exeter. Indeed, in Pembroke's survey of 1567 are listed some very influential people who held large estates in the Longcombe and Yalbourne area, including the influential Kirkhams.

As in Varwell's little house at Brixham, at Longcombe the Prince met men of importance, but here of much higher rank and greater significance, who came from far and wide at short notice to discuss extremely important issues and to witness first hand William's pledge to uphold the Protestant faith. This meeting was William's first parliament in England and because of this the cottage has since been known as Parliament House.

If, as so adamantly stated by Paigntonians, the Prince stayed in Paignton on his second night in Devon – of which there is overwhelming evidence – and

Parliament House, Longcombe, Paignton. (*Peggy Parnell*)

not, as stated by William's clergyman, 'in a Gentleman's house at Yalberton Tor', it is more likely that it was in this gentleman's house the Prince was given lunch. This farmhouse in Yalberton Tor has long been known as King William's Cottage.

Peter Varwell, riding on his own pony, escorted the prince throughout this journey and almost certainly it would have been Varwell who related the vivid description of the cottage interior where William had the meal. It must have been a pretty prestigious house, for it is recorded that a large plaster memorial (no longer in existence) hung above the fireplace near where the Prince sat. According to another record the then owner of this house was so proud of the royal visit that he later had a plaster emblem fixed to the ceiling above where the Prince sat, and the present emblem and the cobbled floor are alleged to be the original ones that survived the house fire of 1869.

In King William's Cottage a standard ceiling marker was installed. This often hapenned following a royal visit. (*Peggy Parnell*)

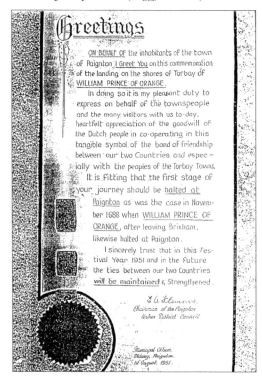

A scroll commemorating the disembarkment of William Prince of Orange at Paignton in 1688.
The original scroll lies deep in Torbay Council's archives.
(*Ernest Britton, PP&LHS*)

No doubt discussions ran on longer than intended and because of this it would have been late in the afternoon before the Prince and his retinue left Yalberton. Huygens, arriving in Paignton, would have been worried at not being able to find the Prince's quarters in the dark, for remember earlier in the day he had been anxious about where the Prince had gone. That evening the Prince did reach the Posting House and the next morning, 7 November, somewhat refreshed, was reunited with his secretary. Together with his lords, nobles, gentlemen and infantry, with Peter Varwell leading the way, they marched first to Newton Abbot where Sir William Courtenay's son had quickly evacuated his home at Ford House so that the Prince and his large retinue could have enough space for the next few days. Here, shortly after the Prince left, the caretaker discovered an engraving of the Prince receiving Sir Edward Seymour of Berry Pomeroy, which almost certainly would have been done by one of Prince William's officers, for his army travelled with everything that was needed, including engravers and his own printing press. Following various upheavals both in Exeter and en route, it took Prince William, escorted throughout by Peter Varwell, around fifty days to meet and greet the populace on his way to London, where Peter received £100 for all his efforts. The rest is history.

In 1951 the then Chairman of the Paignton Urban District Council, Cllr Mrs E.A. Flemmings, presented a scroll relating this story to a contingency of Dutch representatives who were visiting Torbay.

CHAPTER TEN

Oddities

THE SNOOTY END

For some unknown reason, in the early twentieth century the upper part of Well Street was considered the 'snooty end', the middle a little iffy while the Church Street end was decidedly dubious. It's dimly remembered that certain ladies were known as being all right for 3s 6d!

OLD PAIGNTON AND THE DEVON DIALECT

The Revd Mr Lyde-Hunt, a nineteenth-century vicar, was nicknamed 'Lyddy' by the local youth. It is suggested the corruption of this name might have came about because of the Devonian dialect. Certainly the older generation of Paigntonians found it difficult to get their tongues around certain consonants, for example substituting 'v' for 'b' in Devon, thus 'Deb'n', and dropping 'h' in horse – 'orse, or 'yer' for hear and 'b'aint' meaning 'it be not' (which the Oxford English Dictionary considers illiterate). 'In't', is not and 'do'e', do you. 'Yu'd', you would have; 'knaw'd', past tense known; 't, it and the; 'thicky', this; 'wraut', wrote/write; 'prappe'r, proper; 'li'l', little; 'id'n he', isn't he . . . and so it goes on!

A classic example of true Devonian dialect is the story of a visitor to Paignton years ago who, attracted by the watch tower (the Bishop's Tower) at the corner of the restored curtain wall near the church, asked an old man at work in Tower Road what the building was. The road mender pityingly replied, 'Anyone can zee yo b'aint native o' this place or yu'd 'ave know'd t'was in thicky tower David Cawpervield wraut Bible'! (Charles Patterson, *The History of Paignton*, 1952)

TWELVE LONG TABLES

W.E. Couldrey, a well-known local architect of the nineteenth century, could remember in his lifetime one very special event that took place in 1859, which related to the coming of the railway and the activities that marked the great occasion. For generations it had been the custom to hold a feast every fifty years and the chief item on the menu was always a large pudding. At some time this large pudding became a number of small puddings, but in 1859 with the railway about to arrive the good old Paigntonians decided to go one better and produced an enormous one in the shape of a pyramid, 13ft 6in in circumference at the base and 5ft across at its peak. The whole thing weighed half a ton and cost the princely sum of £45. This pud must have been rather like a Christmas cake as it consisted of 573lbs of flour, 191lbs of bread, 382lbs of raisins, 191lbs currants, 382lbs of suet, 320 lemons, 144 nutmegs, 95lbs of sugar, a large quantity of eggs plus 360 quarts of milk. The mind boggles at the size of the oven needed.

Never fear, the resourceful Paigntonians had worked everything out, for it was baked (apparently not boiled) in sections, eight sections to each layer (presumably in different size containers) and once cooked each layer consisted of eight puddings which were built up to form the pyramid. Clever, weren't they? The secret of its cooking was that the sections were baked in the commercial ovens of Evans & Sons, then a popular family bakery in Torbay Road.

The menu for this event also included 1,900lbs of meat and 1,900lbs of bread plus an unlimited supply of that staple drink, cider, produced from Paignton's many orchards. The whole idea was to be a feast for the navvies (workmen) and the poor of Paignton, Marldon and Stoke Gabriel, and to these ends twelve long tables were erected on Paignton Green. At midday a procession moved off from Primley and paraded through the town. By all accounts it was magnificent, headed by a local band with the navvies, their picks and shovels in hand, leading the way, followed by three horse-drawn wagons full of bread, the roast beef following behind in two more wagons, each drawn by two horses. Next came the cider, also pulled by two horses, and last of all came the pudding which because of its tremendous weight was drawn by eight horses. Every wagon was gaily decorated and the air rang with merriment as the committee, carvers and inhabitants walked alongside. When the procession arrived at the Green, John Robinson – a local printer of broadsheets and tracts – had already set up his press there to print penny souvenirs of both the recipe and programme of the day's events. On the Green an area was cordoned off, around which a huge crowd awaited in anticipation for their share of the feast, perhaps a little too eagerly. Just as the cooks started to serve up, the 18,000 hungry onlookers suddenly surged forward and broke down the roped area. The navvies, thinking they were missing out, arose from their privileged seats and joined in the great push along with everyone else, including the police. The carvers became alarmed at the menacing attitude of the crowd so began to slice the meat as fast as they could, throwing it in all directions among the crowd. All hell broke loose until every morsel was gone! Mr Couldrey records that following the incident many people suffered nightmares.

The tradition of a Paignton pudding goes well back into antiquity and there have been many made over the decades. One very special occasion was in 1918, almost certainly to celebrate the end of the First World War, when a huge 'Viggy' pudding was made weighing 900lbs.

Is it any wonder Paigntonians were called 'Pudding Eaters'!

The Principal Farmer's Daughter

A letter from Mr William Rossiter, farmer and nurseryman, to Hammett Pinhey Esq., Paignton, 2 June 1819, was later printed in the *Paignton News* on 9 December 1967, and read:

Sir,

According to your request when you was at my house and subsequent to what we call our Paignton Charter, the 'Paington Pudding', which took place yesterday which I have forwarded you a part of it, you will see there is one part of it red and another part of it white. It was mixed by the principal farmer's daughter of Paington and consisted of four hundredweight of dry flour, one hundred and eighteen pounds of raisins, fourteen pounds of currants, fifty-eight of beef suet, sixty dozen eggs and five gallons of brandy, and was sixty-four hours boiling, which in our opinion was fourteen hours too many, as the middle parts of the pudding is that which is red. It was drawn on a wagon by sixteen large oxen of the true Paington breed with one fine horse to connect the shafts. The wagon horse and oxen were decorated with oak, laurel and garlands of flowers and flags of colours with different inscriptions. On the fore oxen's yoke were these words 'Briton's Glory', on the hind one 'God speed the plough'.

The procession was really grand; it was first drawn round the town, from thence to the sands and divided to about 8,000 people. It was regulated with the greatest economy as everyone who applied partook of a part and the procession continued to great satisfaction of the beholders, many of whom came twenty miles and upwards. I am sorry to say the piece of pudding is not so handsome as I could wish as when it was cut from the cloth it would not keep together, so much for the pudding.

Sir I have sent you a small jar of clotted cream, which I hope will arrive to hand while it is sweet.

I remain sir, your humble servant, Wm Rossiter.

WITH A MIND OF HIS OWN!

After their supper the young men of a well-known farming family used to relax in front of the parlour fire and, gently drawing on their pipes, retell their favourite yarns. One in particular was about a brother who had a horse trained to pull the fire engine, housed just along the road in Well Street. So well trained was this horse that at the sound of the laundry hooter the farmer quickly unfastened its harness, opened the gate and let the stallion streak off madly in the direction of the fire station. Says one of the lads:

> Y'd nay credit what that there 'orse o' mine did t'other day. Remember that there fire at top of street and bells ringing everywhere? Well afore I'z unleashed the gate he'd clear jumped it and there t'was, the zilly bugger 'e one zide and cart on t'other!

Unknown to the storyteller, Mother, having heard it all before, would be standing in the doorway mouthing every word!

A PASSING REMARK

By the mid-1930s the old settlement of Paignton had spread to the top of Marldon Road almost into the village of Marldon. High on the hillside among the cluster of fine pine trees a new estate was just being started and the developer's first house was in its final stage of completion. The builder stood chatting to the lady who was in the process of buying a property and said that he didn't quite know what to call his new road. The lady, looking up at the tall elegant pine trees, suggested, 'Why not Pines Road?' 'What a brilliant idea,' replied the builder and next morning promptly cut all the trees down!

CHAPTER ELEVEN

Near Disasters

THANKS FOR THE HOLY WELL

Of the many disasters that occurred in Paignton, the most outstanding was in 1927 when a fire gutted a row of thatched cottages next door to the Globe Inn in Winner Street and threatened the whole area. The buildings were so badly damaged they were demolished and replaced in the 1920s with modern flats and shops.

The Globe fire might not have been so serious had it not been for a drought that lasted nearly two years (1925–7). With the water restriction in Paignton so severe at the time, permission was given for the local firemen to draw water from the pump house in Well Street, the old 'Holy Well' that never dried up. Thankfully soon after this a new reservoir at Swincombe was built, but the restrictions on the well's use by the fire brigade remained until taken over by the South West Water Board.

HIGH WATER

The town's old Holy Well could cause many a problem, for the water flowed as an open watercourse into Duck Street (now Princes Street) and on into the millpond, its power originally turning the Bishops' waterwheel before flowing on into the marshes and beyond to the sea. Eventually it was connected to the sewer under Littlegate Road and for many years, until larger drains were installed, heavy rainstorms caused flooding in Littlegate Road, as did the severe thunderstorm of 4 August 1938 when the water level reached the upper rooms, leaving a watermark that remained until long after the Second World War.

BEN HUR

Some scalding hot water was very nearly the cause of a terrible disaster. A young Paignton boy related the story about one of the two Pelosi brothers, George and Peter, who used to live in the old cottage in front of the Marist Convent in Fisher Street (long since demolished for housing). Peter and his brother were the sons of an Italian who came to England just before the First World War and was interned here, but eventually settled in Paignton.

This small boy was making his way along Winner Street when he heard the clanging of a loud bell approaching at great speed behind him. It couldn't be anybody else but Peter Pelosi and his ice-cream cart. Peter had recently acquired

Peter Pelosi's ice-cream cart. (*T. Moss*)

a beautiful horse, which he bought from the Army surplus stores at the end of the First World War. It was an exquisite animal with a stamp on its rump, and may well have once been a racehorse for it certainly moved very fast.

The boy, having by now reached the junction of Winner Street and Church Street, was wondering why the ice-cream bell was being rung so vigorously and for so long, and why was Peter driving the horse at such a furious gallop, when suddenly horse and cart turned sharply into Church Street with Peter still ringing and shouting. Later the lad learned that it was for a very good reason.

Peter, having just entered his front door, found his wife bathing the children, steam and soapsuds everywhere, when suddenly the baby slipped out of her mother's arms into a scolding hot bath. Grabbing his little daughter, Peter got into his cart and drove the horse as hard as he could. In those days there were no cars, no traffic lights and no halt signs, so like Ben Hur he galloped through the streets, and of course a horse didn't have brakes so it was a case of 'Stand back everybody!' Fortunately nobody was killed and mercifully he got his little girl to hospital and all was well. It was, nevertheless, an experience this five-year-old would never forget. (Extract from Michael Adams' *Memoirs*, 2002)

AT BREAK-NECK SPEED!

A rag-and-bone man was an early nineteenth-century character who used to collect or buy people's unwanted objects. In Paignton the rag-and-bone man was known locally as 'Half-Crown' because he never gave more than 2s 6d for any item. It so happened that Half-Crown had a cellar store next to the clink, which he rented from Mrs Osborne the tailor around the corner in Church Street, and was just finishing sorting through a huge pile of buttons that he had just purchased from her. Meanwhile Alfie Prowse was coming down Primley Hill on a home-made bicycle when suddenly he discovered – no brakes! 'Ah well', he thought, and with hands hard on handlebars enjoyed flying at the speed of sound through Winner Street, Church Street and down into Princes Street, landing right on target – in the middle of Half-Crown's button display!

WOT? NO WHEELS?

The train left Newton Abbot station for Dartmouth at 11.36 a.m. on 7 January 1875. On emerging from Maypole tunnel, the driver suddenly realised that both his front wheels were off the line and immediately applied the brakes, but at 30mph, going down a steep incline, the train travelled on for another mile before coming to a stop right above a 70ft drop into the River Dart!

Later in the same year, instead of slowing down, a train coming into Torquay from Newton Abbot continued at top speed through the station. Terrified, both the driver and the fireman jumped off, leaving the train, packed to capacity with passengers unaware of the impending danger, to continue at full speed through Paignton and Goodrington stations. As luck would have it, on reaching the viaduct at Churston two plate-layers named Purcell and Harley, who fortunately happened to be on the train, realised that something was very wrong and climbed out onto the carriage roof. They crawled along the top of the train until they reached the engine and, finding no driver, brought the runaway train to a halt. These two brave men were duly rewarded by the Railway directors and in addition were presented with a goodly public subscription. One can only guess what happened to the fireman and the driver! (Dymond & White, *Torquay & Neighbours*, 1800)

CHAPTER TWELVE

Cry Fire!

CLANG! CLANG! CLANG!

It was just before the First World War in 1914 that Michael Adams' father took a job in Robert Waycott's factory of undertakers, cabinetmakers, upholstery and blind makers, which was situated between his brother Arthur Waycott's wine and spirit off-licence and the Globe Inn in Winner Street. The factory was approached via a tunnel beside his brother's wine shop. Michael, who also worked there for a while, well remembers the workers assembled in the tunnel, waiting for the factory bell to ring. It was a big hand-operated bell and when thrust backwards and forwards it emitted a loud clang! clang! clang! This could be heard not only by the staff, but also for miles around, and because of this, between the

Well Street, where the old fire engine was kept. (*Herald & Express*)

workers' arrival and departure, it doubled as the firm's fire alarm. The horse-drawn fire engine around the corner in Well Street, which Michael remembered as a small lad, was quickly manned by voluntary youth who mustered as soon as they could. How those horses knew the difference between a bell rung for the staff in the morning and the same bell being rung for the fire appliance at some other time in the day is a complete mystery! The town's main fire alarm was the laundry hooter in Totnes Road, next to Hayes Road School. (Extract from Michael Adams' *Memoirs*, 2002)

A FINE SWEEP OF BUILDINGS LOST

On 5 July 1952 a violent fire broke out in the town centre. Even Paignton's large reservoir couldn't save the established family firm of Waycotts, who having moved away from their furnishing and brewery activities in Winner Street some years earlier, had ventured into the property market in the new development called Victoria Street, opening an estate agent's business on what became known as Waycotts Corner. The fire spread into Maynard's sweet shop next door, Purdy's tobacconists and Brounette's gown shop along Dendy Road. The damage, not only from the fire but also from the quantity of water used, weakened the walls so badly they had to be pulled down for safety reasons. The attempt to rebuild was unfortunate as it didn't replace the two little-known architects', Hyame & Hogben's, original design, and consequently the focal point to their fine sweep of buildings in Victoria Street was lost.

Hyame & Hogben's grand sweep of buildings in Victoria Street, Paignton. (*T. Moss*)

THE GRAND DUCHESS

In 1938 a local businessman bought a 1929 Wolseley car with a mileage of 1,300 miles for £25, complete with five new tyres. It was big enough for two small boys to fight on the floor when being taken for an afternoon run. The old Duchess, as she was called, could reach 50mph with no effort so at the outbreak of the Second World War, with towing vehicles being in short supply and the grand old car having such a powerful engine, its owner – a leading fireman in the local fire service – offered his car to pull the fire pumps whenever needed. Not convinced, the firemen challenged the car's ability. Equally determined to prove its power, the fire officer arranged to drive it up steep St Mary's Hill loaded to capacity, with firemen standing on the running boards. 'When I say jump off, you jump.' The lads did as they were told. The old car, with no effort at all, reached the top complete with all the firemen. After the war it was sold to Afton Farm for £50, and ended its days as a tractor!

THE VERY LATEST MODEL

Paignton's old steam-operated fire engine was eventually moved from Well Street to the newly erected fire station behind Winner Street, where the young

The old steam fire appliance, replaced in the 1920s. (*T. Moss*)

volunteer firemen in their spare time polished any brass and copper – seen or unseen. The horses that pulled the engine were stabled at the back of the Oldenburg Inn near the old Torbay Mill Seed Merchants, where the Palace Theatre now stands. In the 1920s this grand old machine was replaced with the very latest state-of-the-art Leyland engine complete with solid tyres. Whenever the fire hooter went off young boys would appear from nowhere and follow this new, fast-moving machine. These lads were so keen to see the machine in action that they would follow it for miles. In their eagerness to keep up they often fell, obtaining badly cut knees and hands in the process, but, with blood still flowing, they continued the chase undaunted.

Drilling On The Green

After Victoria Park was completed in the 1930s firemen held their drill practice on the Green between the stream and Hyde Road entrance. One exercise was learning to dress and undress as quickly as possible; another was using the hose which meant learning to handle the heavy nozzle as they ran across the Green and at a given moment shout 'Water!' The pressure at which the water gushed out was so strong they needed all their strength to handle the nozzle and keep it steady on a specially set up target. So difficult was this that a competition was created with a cup awarded for the greatest number of hits, presented to the winner for one year; however, if a fireman won the competition three times he kept the cup. These men joined the fire brigade in addition to their everyday jobs and could be on call at any time. As soon as the laundry hooter sounded they dropped what they were doing and, clambering into their gear, would be off in the fire appliance in the direction of whatever fire was raging. The social life of these chaps had to be suited to their unsociable hours so they set up a special club in their new fire station (now Connections) behind the Palace Theatre. The two highlights of the year were the children's Christmas parties and their annual Firemen's Ball, held in the nearby Public Hall (Palace Theatre).

Icy Water

In 1940 during the Battle of Britain in the Second World War a plane was badly damaged and came down off Paignton pier. Paignton's fire brigade was on the esplanade only moments after it crashed. One of the officers, Francis Down, realising the passengers were in imminent danger, quickly tied a rope to himself and swam out in the ice-cold water, and in so doing saved the lives of all on board. For this courageous deed he was awarded the George Medal, the highest honour the Fire Service could give him. This valiant man went on to win many more awards before the war ended.

CHAPTER THIRTEEN
Early Tourism

A GRAND OLD ALEHOUSE

On Paignton seafront once stood a fine old house, clearly marked on Benjamin Donne's map of 1765 as the Torbay Alehouse, which with the exception of Kirkham House was thought at this time to be the oldest and largest house in Paignton. However, in about 1808 it is written in an untitled document that William Shard and later his wife Mary (William being closely connected with the Shards of Kittery Court, in Kingswear), built a mid-Georgian house on the shoreline, but it is well known that a large house already existed on this site: in 1525 Henry VIII's librarian, John Leland, made note of it while crossing the bay and later wrote, 'I mark almost in the middle of the bay one house set on the hard shore and a small peere by it as a socour for fishchar boats.' When Torbay

The only known photograph of Torbay House. (*Herald & Express*)

House was demolished in 1878 the foundations were discovered to be of very ancient origin, and to this day lie partly under the mini golf course and partly under the Apollo Cinema. It is considered that the site may have been a place of refreshment for seafarers from time immemorial and surely must have been used by the bishops when visiting their ecclesiastical centre. It would therefore seem much more likely that the Shards modernised an existing building that was perhaps deteriorating badly, which is not too surprising if it dated from the mid-sixteenth century and had had any connections with the bishops, for this was the Reformation period when everything to do with the Papists was either sold off or allowed to rot away.

During the Shards' ownership Torbay House was still known as an alehouse, but it was never registered as such and records at this time show only one registration of an alehouse – that being the Ship Inn in Winner Street (better known today as the Oldenburg), which appeared in the Churchwarden's Accounts for the relief of the poor in 1765. In September 1871 the *Exeter Flying Post* advertised the sale of Torbay House and a very fortuitous advertisement it was, for it enables us to peep inside this imposing building before a developer (Mr Fletcher) pulled it down in order to create the present promenade and green. Before the house's demise residents or visitors walking or riding in a fine brougham, or a simple horse and cart, along the rough Town Bank Road (Torbay Road) would have perceived marshes and sand dunes stretching away on either side, while ahead in the distance, slightly to the right, they would have seen a huge building with a high archway spanning a pair of handsome wrought-iron gates that hung between two finely cut granite stone pillars. Later, when the house was demolished, Mr Dendy, another of Paignton's first developers, purchased these pillars to grace the entrance of his new property called Parkfield House in Lower Polsham Road, almost opposite the Redcliffe Tower (now Redcliffe Hotel). The pillars have endured but the beautiful wrought-iron gates have long since vanished.

The whole edifice of Torbay House was set in 5 acres of ground with a large sheltered lawn. The main frontage of the building faced east onto the sea, and it was here a flight of white marble steps could be seen leading up into an entrance porch high above the waterline. On the south side a garden abutted the house, well protected from the east winds and rough sea by a high wall so that in midsummer the perfume of many scented plants filled the air for, according to the late Arthur Evans, lemon verbena, wisteria and other delicate plants flourished here as did a profusion of the most succulent fruits.

Once through those imposing gates into the grounds of Torbay House, any visitor would have immediately become aware of the grandeur of this building, with its two large wings facing partly onto the marshes and partly towards Torbay Road. Following the drive round to the front of the building, visitors would then have had to climb those graceful white marble steps into a neo-Classical porch, beloved of the mid- to late Georgian era, set at first floor level, above which was an impressive balcony, graced on either side with Regency bow windows, all well out of reach of any rough sea. On reaching the entrance at the top of the marble steps, they would have come to a grand but sturdy doorway, probably made of mahogany, with another inner finely etched glass panelled door and then, probably tugging at a blue willow-patterned bell-pull, they would have waited for a housemaid or butler to open the door and invite them in. As they stepped through the entrance the maid or butler would have taken their visiting cards and outer garments, their luggage being left on the drive for the hall porter. They would now have time to weigh up their surroundings and as they walked through the vast hall, with its grand wooden doors which led into the dining room, the breakfast room and a large salon, where one of those attractive bow windows, with a balcony looked out over the south-facing garden. According to the unnamed source of information, several of the rooms had similar bow windows, some with a balcony where people could view from on high in the open air the wonderful scenery, particularly at ebb tide when the surrounding sands were a sight to behold. It was indeed a gracious house with the main rooms running the whole width of the building, with Venetian windows at each end, offering unparalleled views of both the sea and the hinterland that stretched towards the church, the Bishop's Tower and the old town. In the comfort of this luxurious lounge, visitors would have sat supping refreshments and enjoying the wonderful scenery.

On this first-floor level there were six bedrooms adequately provided for with three toilets, and one of these rooms had a small dressing room attached. Above on the second floor was a drawing room that opened onto a library and here, presumably, there were more rooms, though these are not mentioned. Below the first floor, at ground-floor level, were the butler's pantry, the china closet and a large storage room; the servants' hall, an inner kitchen and a large enclosed larder complete with patent 'fly-resistant' wire lattice. Here also was the housekeeper's room with its own Victorian en-suite and nearby were the servants' bedrooms, seven in all. These lower rooms were lofty quarters, being some 8ft high. In addition, typical of a house of this period, there was a strong room for the safekeeping of household plate and valuables. Beneath this again was the basement, which of course was a cool cellar for the storage of wines. There is no mention of what happened when the sea was very rough and penetrated, as it did in 1824! There was apparently another kitchen with scullery, ovens, hot plates and everything required in the running of an establishment of this size, also a granary, shoe house and a large lumber-room situated over the kitchen, which rather suggests that this lower part of the house must have extended out from the main body of the building, perhaps forming part of one of the wings facing Torbay Road. A short distance away from the house was an excellent well, which the agent's advert suggested could be piped into the house at little expense. However, such a grand house as this was not without on-tap water for, like all notable houses in the eighteenth and nineteenth centuries, installed somewhere in the residence were four large rainwater cisterns, which could mean that the Shards rebuilt it to accommodate the rising number of visitors.

Separate from the house were a large laundry, wash-house and scullery with a dairy and arrangements for scalding milk, plus some skillets (large pans) doubtless

This early print of Torbay Alehouse (c. 1820s) was possibly intended as an advert for the Shards' new enterprise. (*Herald & Express*)

for making good old Devonshire cream. Over a double coach house were some servants' quarters with all that was required laid on. The establishment even had its own farmyard, so the alehouse offered their residents fresh milk, eggs, chicken, home-cured ham and, of course, Devonshire cream. All this was probably produced in the outbuildings that can be seen in the photograph (page 91) on the northern side of the old alehouse on Paignton shoreline.

In 1952 there still were iron hinges wedged in the remains of the old boundary wall facing the sea, where a gate once opened from the garden onto the sands. Unfortunately the garden here was without shrubs or flowers because of the salty east winds, and no doubt the intruding sea and sand in the winter months meant that nothing except sea grass grew. However, this easterly aspect was not all desolation, for the grassy area behind the sea wall was used for the popular pastime of archery and during the summer months, in the heyday of Victorian Paignton, grand events such as flower shows, garden parties, tennis, races and donkey rides are known to have been held here. Also in this area was a fine pool, apparently drained and refilled regularly with fresh water by means of a forcing pump.

It was probably because of the Napoleonic wars in the late 1790s and early 1800s that tourists, shunning the French beaches, began to investigate the south and south-west coasts of Britain, seeking out suitable watering places to stay, and one may rightly guess that Mr and Mrs Shard had an eye to business when they took on the old house, so perhaps the drained and refilled pool was a residents' 'plunge pool'. If not, it would have made a very good birdbath, for seagulls of course! An indication that this was Paignton's very first guesthouse is perhaps suggested by the fact that at each end of the old boundary wall facing the sea there were two bathing machines and a boathouse. There was also an old gateway leading onto the beach, neither of which ppear on the photograph on page 91.

It would seem, according to the records found so far, that the Shards must have converted the old sixteenth-century building into a grand guesthouse for those early beach-seeking visitors to Paignton. Perhaps it was the number of early visitors, and the vast amount of land that could be made available if the marshes were drained and levelled, that gave the locals the idea of a purpose-built 'watering place', out of which was born the plan for a tourist town. Even as the unknown writer wrote, he witnessed residents taking up sand at 3d a load and returning a load of earth to help the levelling-up process. Not so long after this a 'For Sale' advert appeared in the local press, and the property was sold to the Seale family of Mount Boone in Dartmouth.

A lithograph depicting the setting of Torbay House following the arrival of Brunel's railway in 1859. (*Herald & Express*)

Very soon two developers took up the challenge of reclaiming the sand dunes and marshes, but one of the developers discovered the sand dunes were generally considered common land, which meant that building on them would lead to serious problems. Because of this a developer, Mr Maclean, who had purchased a considerable amount of foreshore, gifted his rights on Polsham Green to the Local Board. At about the same time Mr Fletcher, a developer from Birmingham, acquired the old alehouse in order to pull it down and create his grand seafront plan, using the stone from the edifice to build Adelphi Terrace.

Torbay House was no ordinary house, and during the various stages of its existence it must have been a veritable oasis among the sand dunes and marshes. Over hundreds of years it must have afforded a welcome sight to any visitors arriving by land or sea in such a barren area.

MORE ABOUT ALEHOUSES

The earliest record of an alehouse establishment in Paignton is in the Earl of Pembroke's survey of 1566, where it is stated there was an establishment called 'Brewhouse' laying next to 'a burgage in Wynerde Street (Winner Street) in Peynton'.

By 1780 the number of licensees had risen to five, which included the Church House and possibly Smokey House in Marldon, although in 1871 records show there were only three people holding a victualler's licence and it apparently stayed that way for another fifty years. In addition to these official houses there were numerous unofficial outlets where tenants provided cider and beer in addition to their normal trade. An example is Samuel Reynolds who kept a beer house and sold refreshments while carrying on his livelihood as a fisherman. His cottage eventually became the Torbay Inn in Fisher Street.

Before alehouses, in the fifteenth century there were long houses or church houses, which provided a meeting place for people where church ales were held and parishioners could partake in them as well as dancing, playing skittles or generally making merry; even cockfighting took place. Basically the whole thing was a way of raising church funds, with the churchwardens providing ales and parishioners donating provisions, much the same as today. In addition, apart from the church ales there were celebration ales like 'bride ales', to give newlyweds a good start, which were probably the forerunner of today's wedding receptions. In addition there were the 'bid ales' to help people overcome difficulties such as bereavement, and the 'Whitsun ales' for the relief of the poor. Unfortunately, in 1603 James I prohibited plays, feasts, banquets, suppers and the taking of church ales in the vicinity of any church, chapel or churchyard. Eventually everything was banned and many old church houses were converted to other uses, such as almshouses or schools, although some later became inns. In Paignton it is thought the Palace Place Social Club could well be what is left of the town's old Church House. By 1617 alehouses were firmly established and many are still in use today under one title or another.

CHAPTER FOURTEEN

Strange Things

A TROPHY OF WAR

An interesting piece of old geological Paignton was uncovered a number of years ago, when at the rear of 20 Winner Street (now no. 173) a passageway leading into the rock face was found. For many years locals thought it led up to the monastery on the hill behind, but the passage is of much older origin, whereas the monastery was built in 1883. The passage, approximately 6ft high by 2ft 6in wide, was discovered situated to the left of an even older seventeenth-century building. At the time there was no record of how far the passage penetrated or what it might have been used for. There was also a further mystery, for the then owner of this property found a cannonball embedded in one of the walls; it had been there so long that when touched it disintegrated. Whether fired or

Chard Bros store in Winner Street. At the back of this store was Mr Deller's Cottages. (*Peter Tully's* Pictures of Paignton Part II, *Obelisk, 1992*)

built into the wall and who put it there will now never be known. Perhaps a French marauder fired it; on the other hand it could simply have been a trophy of war.

In the mid-1940s a Mr Arthur Ward came to Paignton and rented a cottage in one of the old Winner Street courts called Deller's Cottages from Mr Batten, the builder on the corner of Clifton Road and Winner Street. The entrance to these cottages was up an alleyway leading onto Winner Hill, opposite New Street, behind Deller's grocery store (later Chards). All the cottages were occupied except the first one, which was condemned. Because of this Arthur was offered the property for 10s a week. In about 1950 he set up an antiques and furniture repairing business and found it difficult hulking large pieces of furniture up the dangerous steps to his cottage. In addition the only light and heat he had was one gas lamp and one gas ring downstairs, and nothing upstairs – although there was water available from a communal tap outside. Eventually Arthur moved to the end of Winner Street near the junction of Winner Hill Road where he opened his antique shop, and as with the previous tenant soon discovered the old passageway. The stories he heard were that it led to the parish church, but he thought it much more likely to have been used for smuggling.

On venturing further in Arthur discovered a huge cavern. Perhaps this was the secret hideout of those ghostly riders who once sped silently in the dark across Goodrington marshes with illegal cargoes of rum. Perhaps it was the law enforcement officers who fired the cannon ball found by the previous tenant, to rout them out! (Ernest Britton, *The Oldenburg Hotel*, 1990)

ODD COINCIDENCE

Set around the mid-nineteenth century is a story that concerned a man named William Hex who married a Miss Wicks in a shotgun wedding at Stoke Gabriel in 1829. They then took up residence in the Globe Commercial Inn (The Oldenburg) in Winner Street, Paignton, and in time produced four children. The business apparently thrived and William took on a fifteen-year-old domestic help named Joanne Gassell. The autumn and winter of 1841 were difficult for the Hex family particularly because of the death of their youngest child. What drama was enacted over the next few months can only be guessed at, but by the following March William had vanished as had Joanne. A month later the Globe caught fire, said at the time to be a case of arson, but the full details of what caused the fire were never uncovered; it remained one of the unsolved mysteries of Paignton. Was it some strange coincidence that many years later a brewery manager by the name of Hext, living at the top of Winner Street opposite the Market Cross and Mr Long's sweet shop, murdered his wife and child? (Ernest Britton, *The Oldenburg Hotel*, 1990)

AN OLD IRON SAFE

A remarkable find took place in the mid- to late 1890s, an incredible ending to an incident some twenty years earlier. Mr Dendy with his wife and daughter were on their schooner off the coast of Holland when their boat struck a rock and was wrecked. Luckily the occupants managed to escape, but with the exception of a valuable violin everything was lost. On board the yacht was an iron safe which contained gold and silver coins, a quantity of plate, Mrs Dendy's jewels and some valuable papers.

Twenty years later Mr Eastley, the family's solicitor in Paignton, received a letter from the English Consul in Holland enquiring whether Mr or Mrs Dendy or their daughter were still alive and whether they resided in Paignton, as an iron safe had been picked up. On being opened it was found to belong to Mr Dendy. The most amazing thing is that despite the safe having been immersed in water for more than twenty years, its contents were dry and in a perfect state of preservation. Unfortunately, by this time all three members of the family were deceased.

No Great Fuss

Like any town Paignton has had its fair share of mysteries. In particular is a little-known incident that happened sometime between 1924 and 1925. It concerned a Mr Lodder who came to live in Bay View House, one of the fine Georgian villas at the west end of Winner Street. In those days the gardens came down to the pavement with a wide gate and a sweeping drive curving up to the front door. The house is now divided into flats with a row of shops in front of it. A local named Michael Adams knew the house well as his father did odd jobs for Mr Lodder. The previous occupants had been the Hon. Mr Arbuthknott and his family who used the house as a summer residence, and although they were seldom seen, it is recalled that his lads often appeared in kilts. After Mr Arbuthknott and his family left Mr Lodder took over the house as a nursing home; he was the cook and his wife the matron. It was rumoured that he had an American degree in something. Apparently he was an extraordinarily large man, not tall but wide with very fair hair and a full face rather like Henry VIII.

Every day at a regular time he would walk in stately fashion, silver knobbed cane and mail in hand, down the steep drive into Winner Street to a letterbox in the wall by the Oldenburg. On this particular day he was seen to leave the house, but he never returned! Very strange, for as far as it is known nobody reported him missing, there was no public enquiry and no great fuss was made about his disappearance. A few people kept a lookout for him, particularly along the beaches and in the coves. However, it was well known that his wife had recently died and that he was heavily in debt. He was left with just the matron to run the home and no money to provide for the patients. Within a matter of months and without any explanation he was presumed dead, but even stranger still his affairs were suddenly cleared up, the property sold and nothing more was heard of him. To all intents and purposes he had simply vanished from the face of the earth! (Extract from Michael Adams' *Memoirs*, 2002)

CHAPTER FIFTEEN

Ghosts

ROOM 65

During the early hours of the morning of Sunday 14 December 1971 a CID officer staying at the Redcliffe Hotel awoke to see a figure standing in his room. It was a lady of about thirty-five years of age, about 5ft 5in tall, wearing a plain dark red, full-length dressing gown, tied around her middle with a cord. She had light brown hair, worn as a long plait, which was slung over her left shoulder and down her front. There was neither noise nor unusual atmosphere as the officer watched her walk slowly across the room and disappear through an internal wall!

The mere fact of her disappearing through a wall suggested to the officer, without any doubt, that she was a ghost, and the only one the officer had ever seen! His personal theory was that she had walked through Room 65 many times, but on this occasion something may have attracted her, possibly some coins on a shelf which she simply wanted to have a closer look at.

A NICE LADY

When new tenants first moved into Kirkham Cottage before it caught fire for the second time, they learnt this attractive thatched cottage at the corner of Kirkham Street was reputed to be home to strange events. They soon discovered this was true. Odd things were certainly happening, particularly in the Victorian kitchen extension where loud bangs and noises could be heard during the night. In October and November the occupants witnessed pictures being lifted off the wall and plates hauled off the dresser onto the floor. On one occasion they even saw a ball of light the size of a melon, which appeared to hover then vanish, travel across the kitchen. They were terrified, but as time passed found these incidences were not malicious or directed at anybody in particular; rather they felt that the spirit or poltergeist was perhaps seeking attention.

It is said poltergeists are known to have some correlation with children; certainly a previous tenant's little girl, aged four or five at the time, used to tell her mother that a very nice lady came into her bedroom and talked to her. From the child's description the spectre was possibly early Victorian, and aged between thirty and forty. It might be that this lady lost a child in Kirkham Cottage and, as was the practice in the past, the child was buried in the garden at a spot that is now beneath the kitchen extension. In the mid-nineteenth century, without any apparent reason, the cottage burnt down, but was later rebuilt. On Thursday 20 April 2004 fire broke out once again, engulfing the whole cottage. The reason is apparently unknown and one has to ask if there is something more to the ghostly activities in this picture–postcard house?

THE HAUNTED PRISON

Residents living around the area of Paignton's medieval clink say that even on a warm summer's evening a cold atmosphere can be experienced when passing by, and at times even moaning can be heard. Perhaps it's the wind blowing across the old barrel roof. On the other hand, could it be the spirit of an internee who hanged himself from the ceiling in 1860?

A BALMY AUGUST EVENING

For some unknown reason there are strange atmospheres not only in the Oldenburg Inn but also across the lane in the Palace Theatre, for many curious incidents have been recorded in both establishments. One story in particular is that of an old lady sitting alone in the theatre auditorium dressed in winter clothes on a hot, balmy August night. When she was approached by the caretaker she vanished! (Extract from A. Calland, *The Grand Old Lady*, 1986)

THE PUB THAT NEVER WAS

The Oldenburg Inn in Winner Street, like so many old buildings, has a ghost and this one appears at the rear of the building on a certain night in August.

The Duke of Oldenburg, a frequent visitor to Torbay in the 1850s and in particular to Paignton, had a bathing machine on the beach (run by William Ackrell of Yellands) for his family's use. Here he would leave them for the day while he trotted off on his horse to explore the local countryside, always returning to the Globe Inn for his refreshments, probably local roast pork and a tankard of the Globe's best cider. It is thought he sometimes stayed at the Globe Inn (sometimes referred to as a hotel), but it is just possible he could have stayed with Admiral Sherrington who lived in Lower Polsham Road, for it is thought the Admiral's house, like the Globe, was probably renamed Oldenburg following the Duke's accession to his father's realm. The sign over the entrance to the inn still depicts a rider on horseback.

One day a visitor was standing in the lane behind the inn musing on the hotel's history when an old man suddenly appeared at his side and told him that late in the last century his grandfather had stood on this very same spot at about eleven o'clock on a warm August evening. The old man further explained that in those days it was little more than a dusty track with cabbage allotments where the Palace Theatre (Old Public Hall) now stands. The old man's grandfather became aware of a horse approaching from behind and, as it rushed past, felt the brush of a tail but never saw the horse or its rider!

The tourist, with tongue in cheek, enquired, 'Maybe the horse and its rider were shy?'

'Per-haps', replied the old man slowly, 'and perhaps the inn was shy also.'

'What on earth do you mean?' asked the tourist.

'Well, sir,' said the old man, 'have you ever seen a drawing of this inn [the Oldenburg]? Try looking for it and all you will find is a pub that never was.'

'Strange', the tourist thought and turned to enquire further but the old man was gone! Only a few have admitted to this encounter on 22 August or so, for apparently it was the Duke's birthday at this time. Numerous enquiries were made but nothing was ever found, but what was discovered was permission for a new licensed house to be erected on the corner of Windmill and Cecilia Road that was never built; only a drawing by the architect W.G. Couldry survives! (Ernest Britton, *The Oldenburg Hotel*, 1990)

FOOD FOR THOUGHT

An eccentric woman continually left parcels of food in the parish churchyard until the day she was caught opening a grave.

CHAPTER SIXTEEN

Three Old Houses
& A Toffee Factory

Few people in Paignton who travel out of town towards Totnes realise that at the west end of Winner Street, between the junction with Fisher Street and the corner of Conway Road, to the left of Totnes Road, was one of Paignton's earliest cider-making businesses. It had its own orchard, pound house

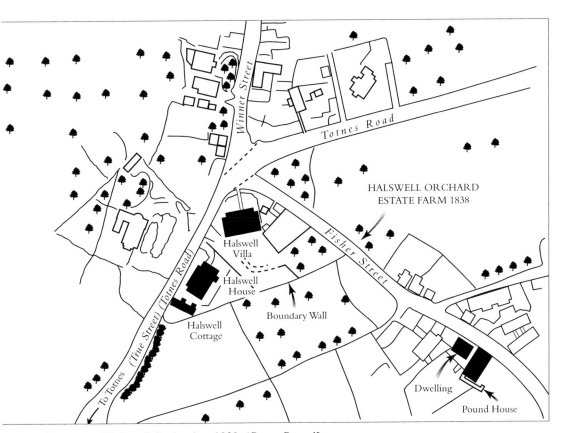

Site map of Halswell Orchard, *c.* 1838. (*Peggy Parnell*)

(cider-press), barn, pump and pump house, and was commonly called Halswell Orchard. On part of the land, before the massive development of this area, three interesting old houses were erected named Halswell House, Halswell Cottage and Halswell Villa.

Around the time of the Napoleonic wars when sea captains regularly put into Torbay, there was an increasing demand for ground to build grand villas on, and land near the coast was eagerly sought after for many fine properties. It is thought that this is when areas such as Halswell Orchard became more valuable as building land than for the production of cider.

There is a suggestion that this site, or part of it, was at some time crown land, but research has not proved or disproved this. However, investigation into this possibility soon revealed some interesting bits of Paignton history. The earliest known document, dated 1749, refers to this site as Halswell Orchard. At this time the land apparently passed between several members of the nobility.

But before this, in 1682, a Totnes merchant named John Kelland held the manor of Paignton. On his death the manor seems to have passed to his son Charles Kelland Courtney, and on Charles' death possibly to his daughter, who became a co-heiress. She apparently married into the family of the Earls of Cork and Orrory, and it is thought later married a William Poyntz.

The documents of 1749 name the Hon. Edmund Monckton, Rt-Hon. Edmund Earl of Cork and Orrory (Lord of the Manor of Paignton) and the Rt-Hon. Edmund Boyle (commonly called Viscount Dungarvan). These documents still contain the name of William Poyntz, but with his wife Isabella, and also there are now a William Stephen Poyntz and a Nicholas Prout Berry, all of whom are mentioned in the transactions of this site. But in 1766 a lease and release was signed between a John Bradford, clerk, Dame Bridget Maria Northcote (indentures show that the Northcotes were co-heirs of Paignton Manor by this time), also Sir Stafford Northcote, Bart, Samuel Pearce and Hugh Northcote, clerk, and Nicolas Berry; a grandson perhaps? Other names mentioned were John Philips, John King, Thomas Hammersley, Wallwyn Shepheard and John Bradford, clerk.

Perhaps it was because of the lords' and all the other nobles' names that the notion of crown land originated. In any case, such a formidable list of aristocracy shows how important the Halswell Orchard site must have been.

HALSWELL HOUSE AND THE ESTATE DWELLING HOUSE

In November 1815 the Revd Robert Bradford of Newton Abbot (possibly the grandson of John Bradford) acquired the freehold of Halswell Orchard. Eight years later, on 12 September 1823, this reverend disposed of Halswell Orchard to various people, the first being a Mr Symons who was already in possession of part, if not all, of the orchard, which he was sub-letting to Mr John King Tozer, a local gardener. On the same day Mr Bradford also sold the stables, court, linhey (an open garden/farm shed) and pumphouse to Mark Hill Gardner for £85, and at the same time he conveyed to John Kestele RN and his wife Jemima the 'messuage dwelling house garden spot of land & premises – formerly a pound house barn & orchard, commonly called Halswell Orchard'. This pound house (cider press) faced onto Fisher Street, where years later Lewis the Builders and later still Harmony Signs operated. Strange as it may seem, the dwelling which stood on the site of the old barn, by now a new house, was also known as Halswell Orchard, as written in the document for Kestele when he made a 'bearing gift' of this property to his wife in 1826.

This tells us that the Halswell Orchard estate had stopped functioning as a cider-producing farm and was being split up. Before this Catherine Berry, the widow of Nicholas Prout Berry, together with John Bradford, had held the land for some years. They are mentioned, together with Mark Hill Gardner, in a 1794 schedule, which suggests these people may well have been the last trustees of the Halswell Orchard estate. Perhaps with the cider business declining, they agreed the Revd Robert Bradford should have the freehold of the Halswell Orchard estate, but perhaps Bradford later found it no longer viable and started leasing out the land. Unfortunately there are no indentures showing the actual dates when the three Halswell properties were erected on the Halswell Orchard estate, who built them or who the first owners were. But it would be very unlikely, with what documentation is available following the transactions made between the Revd Robert Bradford and Mark Hill Gardner in 1823, that anyone other than Mark Hill Gardner would have been involved with building Halswell House. Certainly he and his wife Louisa and their two sons lived there until his death in 1831 when he left everything to his wife. However, shortly before he died he altered his will to form a trust so that his wife Louisa could remain in the house as long as she lived or until she wished to sell.

In 1837 Jemima Kestele also became a widow and requested, within her legal dowry right, to sell up. She was given the option, if she so wished, to keep the house for a short term at a fee and afterwards have permission to use a back bedroom for storage if she so required. She was, however, willing to let go all fixtures and fittings associated with the property, which of course was formerly the pound house barn and orchard called Halswell Orchard; however, by this time a new house had been built. She duly conveyed the property to Mr Henry Browse, except for a piece of land at the west end of the orchard adjoining Mrs Gardner's wall, next to the Turnpike (Totnes Road) and 25ft towards Mrs Symons' orchard. Mr Browse then requested that an 8ft high boundary wall 18in thick, consisting of lime, sand and stone, be erected across the orchard at the joint expense of himself and Mrs Gardner. This boundary wall, which can still be seen, cut Louisa Gardner off from most of Halswell Orchard, which was originally open land between the Kesteles and the Gardners. The sum paid by Mr Browse for this newly divided land, including the house called Halswell Orchard, was £1,320.

When Louisa Gardner died in 1869 her son, Henry John Gardner, now sole executor, sold Halswell House outright to Ann Hill Eastley, the widow of a well-known local solicitor Captain Charles Eastley. At the same time he sold the cottage leasehold, which included the old court and outhouse, to the then occupier Jane Palk.

From then on Halswell House passed through numerous leaseholds, eventually becoming freehold in the hands of a well-known Paigntonian, H. Bond Esq., and interestingly in his indenture of 29 March 1952 there was a mention of a property immediately behind Halswell House, formerly belonging to the well-known Revd Finney Belfield. (See Halswell Tithe Map on page 4)

Possibly due to the complex set-up that had developed over the years, or maybe because of the Landlord and Tenant Act of 1980, after the last resident in Halswell House – a Mrs Nancy Mudge – left, there appears to have been some problem as the house was boarded up for several years. It eventually became a safe house for women and children at risk.

HALSWELL COTTAGE

When Louisa Gardner was widowed in 1831 she decided to sell off the linhey, court and stables, but because of the trust arranged by her husband she was unable to sell even though everything belonged to her, so she sought the Trust's permission to sell these buildings for £18 with a proviso: 'he' [thought to refer to John. R. King Tozer, local gardener/builder] does not default during the life of the executors', whatever this may have meant, but the Trust refused and it was six years before Louisa Gardner got her wish to dispose of the buildings. An agreement was finally drawn up between Louisa Gardner, John Kestele RN and John Jackson Goodridge, surgeon, and John R. King Tozer, the executors of Mark's last will, who were all paid the customary 5s to clinch the deal, and with the transaction receipted John K. Tozer purchased the linhey, court and stables next to Halswell House. Shortly after this, on 15 October 1837, John Kestele died. The transactions that followed are somewhat complicated and it is thought Louisa Gardner gave J.R.K. Tozer permission to clear the site, which he did, but then he started to dismantle the linhey and stables and erect a cottage. While carrying out the work there seemed to be a great deal of wrangling between the builder and the Trustees, causing a considerable number of signed documents to be produced. By 1837, in place of the linhey, court and stables there now stood a cottage built in the style of Halswell Villa; oddly, this site with its new building was back in the possession of Louisa Gardner! It would appear she bought the site back once the building was completed. This could have been a kind of transaction often undertaken before bank loans, a way of raising funds for the builder. The huge amount of documentation involved in the building of this cottage, too much to elaborate upon here, may have been in part owing to the well and pump house, which apparently was near the linhey and stables. Perhaps the original name of this waterhole was 'Hor' or 'Holy' well, from which the site and the three old houses acquired their name, but the records don't go back far enough to prove or disprove this theory. However, one thing is for sure: over the generations practically everybody who was anybody in Paignton had their name on one or other of the documents relating to Halswell House and Halswell Cottage, including the Eastleys, the Goodridge-Lidstones, the Hills, the Gardners, the Mudges and the Kesteles, all of whom seem to have some connection with one another as the same names

Halswell Cottage, Totnes Road. (*Peggy Parnell*)

keep occurring through the years as executors, trustees and even, it would seem, possibly part owners.

There is a legend that sometime during the 1860s or possibly later in the early twentieth century Halswell Cottage become famous when a well-known local business couple called Pollybank moved in with their large family of girls. Their eldest daughter improved her family's status, so it is said, by marrying a member of the D'Oyley Carte family of Gilbert and Sullivan fame. However, research has proved nothing conclusive.

The interior of Halswell Cottage is a delight and one feature in particular is a very fine wooden banister-rail carved out of one piece of timber said to have come from HMS *Victory*. A dubious claim perhaps, but it is a fact that in 1805, following the Battle of Trafalgar, as was always the practice following any sea battle, all ships large and small, including, of course, Nelson's flagship, were taken into port for a refit. All would have had their damaged and rotten timbers stripped and the wood sold on to the public. In fact the ships all but had a total rebuild. Both the cottage and the villa are said to have HMS *Victory* timbers in them, remarkable considering there is a thirty-two year gap between the two buildings, but of course there would have been a lot of timber available for a long time. But how Halswell Cottage came to be built thirty-seven years later in the style of Halswell Villa is one of the mysteries of Halswell Orchard.

HALSWELL VILLA

Sadly little has been discovered about Halswell Villa, but it is without doubt the earliest of the three old houses, known better to the locals as Regency House because of its fine period work. The only document relating to Halswell Villa dates from 1808 when Mrs Emily May Burton from Sidmouth signed an indenture, and fifteen years later in 1823 she signed its release. It's rather strange that this should be the same year that the Revd Robert Bradford started leasing out the estate, but even so none of the documents investigated show any connection with the villa or its occupants.

According to a recent visitor to the house, it is said to have three ghosts. One is said to be that of a naval officer with a grey beard who, wearing the Royal Navy uniform of the Napoleonic period, is occasionally seen at a window in the attic peering through his spyglass towards the bay, apparently, so it is said, watching his ship go down! Maybe it was one of those great storms that so often hit Torbay? But is this ghost telling us something about the past and is there perhaps a Royal Navy connection? Certainly there is the reputed connection of timbers from Nelson's ship, but many houses built at this time can also make this claim to fame. Was John Kestele RN perhaps related to the people in the villa before he took up residence in the Old Pound House? Unless more documents come to light, the villa's history will never be known.

Whatever the truth, Halswell Villa must surely be linked in some way with Halswell Orchard, as it was in existence long before the estate was split up, but for whom was it built, and why? Perhaps the early date of 1808 is telling us something and a good guess could be for a sea captain, but it could equally have been built for one or other of the Halswell Orchard trustees.

By the 1950s the villa was under threat of demolition for road widening, but the then owner, who was probably unaware of the villa's history but appreciated the age and architecture of the building, had the villa and indeed all three properties registered as Grade II listed buildings. Halswell Villa has been used ever since as a dance studio, but sadly because of this the interior has been considerably altered. It is also said that at some time the old orchard was used as a pig-rearing farm. This is possible, for during the 1930s into the early 1950s a well-known local family called Williams, owners of several butchery businesses in the town, lived in Halswell Villa, known then as Regency House.

Over the years the three old houses have survived, even though Halswell Orchard cider farm has long since disappeared, and their ownership has passed back and forwards through the years between many well-known Paigntonians. But it is thanks to that one gentleman who contacted English Heritage and succeeded in

Halswell Villa and the Toffee Factory, Totnes Road, Paignton. (*Peggy Parnell*)

listing not only Halswell Villa but also Halswell House and Halswell Cottage that these three buildings and their architecture are still with us to this day.

THE TOFFEE FACTORY

Next door to the villa, still on the Halswell Orchard estate, is a much more recent property which, in the 1940s, was operational as Hopkins' Toffee and Boiled Sweet Factory, making fudge and toffees. Behind the shop can still be seen traces of the sweet factory and the old milking sheds. Folk living nearby can still recall dairy cows being brought in and out through the archway to produce the fresh milk required for the factory. During the Second World War many a child on their way to school spent their pocket money in the shop. Today the shop is a rehabilitation centre for people with certain types of illnesses, while the area behind was once the garden of Halswell Villa, which would have already been reduced when Halswell House was built.

CHAPTER SEVENTEEN
The Sea & Ships

MAN OVERBOARD

On 22 May 1800 the Earl St Vincent's fleet was lying in Torbay when an accident occurred on Paignton sands, which arose out of the loss overboard of a £1 note. Six of the ships crew leaped into the sea to recover it and all would have perished in the strong surf had not two privates of Captain Eastley's Volunteer Co., then exercising on the beach, stripped off and swum to their rescue. Five seamen were saved, but the sixth drowned. (Extract from Dymond & White, *Torquay & Neighbours*, 1800)

A BID FOR FREEDOM

In March 1784 a ship with nearly 200 convicts on board arrived in Torbay from London, bound for Baltimore. The prisoners had ten days earlier risen against the master and crew and, having got drunk, caused the vessel to drift towards the shore. One hundred and sixteen of them landed at Paignton and managed to escape; forty more made a similar attempt but were captured by various boats before reaching the shore and taken to the high gaol at Exeter, while several more were later rounded up. Twenty-four were tried at a special Assize set up for the purpose in Exeter before Mr Justice Heath. (Extract from Dymond & White, *Torquay & Neighbours*, 1800)

SHOULD THE FRENCH ATTACK

At a meeting held in the Crown and Anchor Inn, Paignton, in 1802 it was resolved that the infirm and children under the age of eight years who were incapable of walking ten miles in one day should, in the case of alarm of enemy attack, be assembled in three divisions, namely Torquay, Tor and Upton. It was also recommended that those people who were not employed in any particular service should, at the raising of an alarm, go immediately to the Revd Mr W. Kitson at the church, 'to consult in what manner they can render the greatest assistance to their neighbours and their country – Signed W. Kitson, Superintendent'. (Extract from Dymond & White, *Torquay & Neighbours*, 1800)

GREAT STORMS

In the seventeenth century Torbay was recommended as a safe anchorage to ships, being one of the most suitable bays to shelter in while fleets were assembled.

Rough sea off Corbyn Head. (*Roy Authors*)

Because of this the East India Co. sailed their first ships out of the bay on 2 May 1601. Throughout the eighteenth and nineteenth centuries the bay became a popular rendezvous for Channel-plying ships but many soon discovered that, although sheltered from the west, the bay is exposed to severe gales and over the years countless ships were blown onto the rocks around Torbay. One classic occasion was in 1745 when a fleet sheltering in the bay was caught in a severe storm. The admiral was endeavouring to get his fleet underway when a south-easterly wind strengthened, causing a great swell. Many ships dragged their anchors and cut their cables, which threw the fleet into chaos. The *Royal George*, one of the East India ships en route for Africa, fouled the coast off Brest and was sunk, but fortunately the crew was saved. Others were forced into Portsmouth to refit, but the *Expedition* to Lisbon was driven onto Berry Head and bilged. Fortunately all the crew and part of her cargo were saved, but the *Tiger*, making for Newfoundland, was not so lucky – she also finished up on Berry Head with the loss of 170 soldiers, six sailors and six women, while the captain broke both legs scrambling onto the rocks. Other ships were badly damaged by a man-o-war running loose. This was reported in the *Gentleman's Magazine* of 1745, which clearly portrays what happened many times in the days of high-masted ships in Torbay.

RELUCTANT TO HELP

On 24 November 1804, during the Napoleonic wars, as Admiral Cornwallis's fleet was leaving Torbay for its station off Brest, the *Venerable*, being the rearward ship, missed its stays (ropes) and was wrecked off Goodrington. There was little wind, but a heavy swell was breaking onto the shore and the ship became totally unmanageable. Even with her masts cut away, she was still driven onto the rocks at Paignton Ledge and here the sea finished her off. Eight of her crew were drowned, the rest saved by boats that put out from Paignton, Brixham and Torquay. Bystanders on the shore were reluctant to help, no doubt in anticipation of the salvage, but for the crew of HMS *Impeteux* even more would have drowned. Fortunately the Paignton Volunteers arrived and managed to save some of the ship's stores from being pillaged.

Later at the court-martial the captain and crew were honourably acquitted except for one marine who, because of some improper behaviour following the shipwreck, was ordered to receive 200 lashes from ship to ship round the fleet! (Extract from Dymond & White, *Torquay & Neighbours*, 1800)

A BRAVE ESCAPE

A well-known story relates to a William Adams who was born in Paignton in 1612, of mean and obscure parentage. At the age of twenty-seven he decided to go to sea and sailed from Gravesend in the company of several others en route for the West Indies. They had been at sea only a few days when they were taken captive by a Turco man-of-war and carried off to Algiers where they endured five years of miserable captivity.

After a lot of thinking and talking, William and several of his cell-mates decided to attempt an escape and quietly set their plans in operation, secretly fitting out the model of a boat in sections, planned in such a manner that they could fit everything together as quickly as possible. They managed to obtain a piece of wood 12ft long to serve as a keel and cut it into two so as not to attract attention; they then joined it at the middle and fitted the ribs, finally covering the whole with canvas. Two staves from a barrel served as oars. On 30 June 1644, with some bread and two leather bottles of water, William Adams, John Jeffs, John Anthony, John the carpenter (his name is not recorded) and William Oakley made their escape.

Four of them continually rowed while the fifth bailed out. But the salt water soon spoiled their bread and in a matter of three days they were faced with starvation. After five days they abandoned all hope of survival and ceased rowing, although they continued bailing out.

As luck would have it the currents were in their favour and they drifted towards Majorca where they were found dehydrated and weak. Here they were cared for by those who found them, and when recovered they were put on one of the King of Spain's galleys to Alicante, whence they returned to England.

William Adams later became a Master Mariner and followed a sea life for many years. He died in 1687 and was buried in Paignton's parish churchyard.

This is a story that illustrates the strong character of West Country seamen in the seventeenth century.

LADIES' LEGACY

Protection at sea had long been necessary even before Grace Darling pulled her father's longboat from his lighthouse on an awesome night in the winter of 1838, when she and her father rowed through a lashing cold sea to rescue survivors from the SS Forfarshire breaking up on the rocks, an action that encouraged the early RNLI to provide more lifesaving boats. Since the 1770s the RNLI had realised the need for a better rescue service in certain areas around the coast of Britain, but it took a tragedy in 1789 at the mouth of the River Tyne before something was done to provide a number of specially equipped boats suitable for saving lives, and it would be 1823, thirty-four years later, before they fully realised the need for a national organisation. One year later on 12 February 1824 an appeal was launched and the embryonic RNLI was fully initiated. Although several boats were designed and built for saving lives, there was a great need to provide even more, but, as always, money was not available for the maintenance and handling of such boats and their equipment. Eventually the RNLI managed to place a number of boats in vulnerable areas, although it was 1866 before Torbay's first boat was installed in Brixham harbour.

In 1927, nine years after the First World War ended, the RNLI decided to replace Brixham's 40ft open boat with its one petrol engine capable of 7 knots, by which time it had been on the station for five years. There was great concern among the locals regarding the huge cost of £9,614 to replace this old boat so they set about raising a subscription towards this hefty sum. Amazingly, one year later they had collected enough to purchase a 37ft Barnet housing two 60hp CE6 engines capable of 9 knots. At the time this would have been considered a state-of-the-art boat with a cabin capable of holding ten survivors, a searchlight and a radio for transmitting Morse signals: a fantastic improvement over that open boat equipped with just a compass.

This action spurred the hearts of several Paigntonians. One in particular, a lady named Mrs Templer, clearly saw the need for a regular income to support the lifeboat and set about rallying a few ladies to help her, and by 10 December 1929 had formed a group that would eventually become the Paignton Ladies Guild of the RNLI.

In those days transport in Paignton was mainly horse and cart, the motor car barely seen except in the hands of the Singer family of Oldway. By 1913 a number of bicycles had started to appear in the area, mainly because of Raleigh of Nottingham who had made cycles before the First World War primarily for tradesmen's use. At the start of the war Raleigh were commissioned to produce bicycles for dispatch riders as well as replacements for units of the army who had already taken on this modern form of transport. After the war Raleigh realised the market potential and began to mass-produce bicycles for general use, so for these young RNLI ladies the bicycle and even the tricycle quickly became the vogue, and there is little doubting that these enterprising ladies, in their short flapper skirts with beads a-dangling, dainty shoes and heads adorned in colourful bands, would have made good use of this new pedal-power. One can just imagine them in their lovely dresses nipping between whist drives, tea dances, tennis parties, sales of work and fêtes on the green with such enterprising competitions as guessing the weight of a pig and tug-o-war, all this as well as putting on various other events in cafés such as Deller's and Evans'. They did so well that by 1931 the guild had expanded to twenty-three ladies who now made house-to-house collections, and even instigated a flag day event raising £202 0s 2d, which of course was sent to the RNLI headquarters. By 1932 they were recruiting new members, each one promptly being given a collection box! At the same time they introduced the idea of annual subscriptions. Another year on saw their first Bridge Drive.

Two years later one of the members became the proud owner of a motor car and made it available for the flag day. In 1937 they held a concert in Palace Avenue, tickets 6d, 1s, 1s 6d and 2s 6d. But then came the Second World War and many of the girls were called up or involved in the war effort; as a result no Annual General Meetings were held. But as soon as the war ended they burst forth with even more vigour, organising and fund-raising. Ladies' fashions by this time had changed to longer skirts, with layers of under-slips, their outfits complemented by mushroom-shaped hats. The great efforts put in by these various Ladies' Guilds prompted the RNLI headquarters to appoint district and area co-ordinators and the introduction of national souvenirs. Now, a generation later, these are still going strong.

CHAPTER EIGHTEEN
Church Tales

A SACRED PLACE

Five old cottages and a barn once stood in Colley End near a natural water outlet used by both man and beast. In 1864 the barn was removed and a huge stone trough was built to collect the water. A later version was a little more elaborate with heavy metal cups on chains decorated in elaborate ironwork and topped with a street lamp. In the 1930s a certain little girl insisted on filling one of the cups with the crystal-clear water that flowed constantly out of a 'gargoyle' tap whenever she passed this trough. In 1936 Paignton's water system was upgraded and this grand fountain-head was removed when the spring was taken over by the Paignton Urban District Council.

Opposite the stone water trough was the first Catholic church and next door were two thatched cottages with a shared small garden, outside loo and a clothes line where, on windy days, washing blew like flags towards passers-by. The first Catholic school (today housing) was built on the land opposite the church, roughly where the old barn once stood. The Catholic church had been the town's first Baptist chapel complete with baptismal bath, which was, after years of neglect, full of unmentionable grime. When the Catholic authorities began converting the chapel one of the workmen called the priest to come and have a look at what he had found. The priest joined him and the workman, lifting the huge lid, pointed to the mess inside the bath, saying, 'Whatever is that at the bottom'?

'Ah!' replied the priest, 'That's original sin!'

TREATS FOR TINY TOTS

Off Colley End is a steep hill known to born and bred Paigntonians as St Mary's Hill. At the top of this hill was once an ancient barrow (burial ground) and it was here the Marist Fathers bought a large house for their seminary. At the pinnacle of their oratory they placed a white statue of the Virgin Mary, which at the time of writing, although white no longer, still stands sentinel over the town. This seminary could also be approached via Winner Hill Road; into the road the locals nicknamed Monastery Road, which has since become its official name. Many of the entrants were eighteen year olds who came from far and wide to study theology. The Marist teaching order came to England in about 1890 with the expulsion of various religious orders following the downfall of Emperor Napoleon in France.

The Marist Fathers' seminary. (*T. Moss*)

At the college entrance was a fine pair of wrought-iron gates with the words 'Marist Fathers' on them; a little less ostentatious was the tradesmen's entrance, approached via Berry Drive opposite the cemetery, also with 'Marist Fathers' on the gate. By 1901 the Marist Sisters had moved into Southfield House where they founded their first Marist Convent School. Several years later the Sisters purchased and moved into Mr Bailey's Tower House in Fisher Street, immediately erecting, in the grounds facing onto Grosvenor Road, a strangely worded title board:

> Marist Convent
> School for the Daughters of Gentlemen,
> and Little Boys

which was subsequently changed to:

> Boarding and Day School for Young Ladies
> Preparatory School for Little Boys

Corpus Christi is a religious festival held in June every year and it was tradition for every Catholic school to have a holiday to celebrate the Feast Day. The Catholic church's annual fête was held for many years in the grounds of

The Marist Convent girls playing on the lawn of their new school in Tower House, 1908. (*Peggy Parnell*)

the seminary (affectionately known as the monastery) by kind permission of the Marist Fathers, but occasionally it was held in the convent grounds and sometimes in Adelphi Park.

Closely followed in June, weather permitting, was the Infant school's outing to Goodrington sands near the Marist Sisters' beach hut. One of the priests would treat all the pupils to ice-creams and triangular bags of sticky pear drops, while Sister Ninian and Sister Oliver sat comfortably in their deckchairs, watching with eagle eye their small charges run in and out of the sea.

A Devonian Twist!

In Colley End there was once a general store run by a well-known lady named Mrs Coombs. After lunch on most afternoons about twenty or so Marist Fathers would walk into town in groups of three dressed in their ecclesiastical black. One day as they were passing the good lady's shop a customer, a stranger to the town, remarked, 'What ever! Has there been an awful tragedy with all those young men going to a funeral?' To which Mrs Coombs in her glorious Devonian voice replied, 'Oh no! Them be from up Catholic, them learning 'em to be fathers!' (Extracts from Michael Adams' *Memoirs*, 2002)

BREAKFAST IN THE VESTRY

One well-known character of nineteenth-century Paignton was the Revd Mr Lyde Hunt who was often the celebrant at weekday Holy Communion in the parish church. Immediately after a service he used to enter the vestry and, before removing his cassock and surplice, he would sat down on the nearest chair and putting hand in pocket retrieve a package. Then, carefully unwrapping it, he proceeded to eat a bacon sandwich!

At another service (a special festival) the same vicar, on this occasion sitting in the congregation, was so impressed with the choir's vocal efforts that he gave each boy 2*d* and promised that if they maintained their standard at the next festival he would give them 4*d*; then when the next festival came around he would give them 6*d*. He never did turn up!

This same clergyman occasionally invited all the choirboys into his garden at Barns Hill House (Efford's Farm), telling them they could have all the fruit they wanted including raspberries and strawberries, but not to touch the fruit!

THE CHOIRBOY PEER

During the early 1900s the choir of Paignton parish church included among its members a peer of the realm called Lord Elibank. One of the young choristers, Bill Coysh by name, recalled as a small boy when His Lordship entered the vestry, Bill would copy the older choir-men and bow very respectfully, greeting

Parish church choir, early 1950s. (*D. Wood*)

him as he passed with 'Good morning, My Lord'. The vestry was so small the choir could barely move so this gesture of respect was quite a feat; nevertheless all managed to bend nearly double. However this peer was not averse, when he considered the occasion demanded it, to using a hymnbook to wallop the head of any boy whom he saw misbehaving in the choir stalls. (Bill Coysh, Arthur Day's article, *Herald & Express*, 1959)

OVERHEARD

The Revd Mr Linzee-Giles, during part of his incumbency, occupied a temporary vicarage in Polsham Park while the present vicarage was being built. At the time it was his custom before a service to enter the church by the west door, walk down the nave and enter the vestry via the chancel door. On one of these occasions he passed a pew where a very old and profoundly deaf lady was sitting and heard her remark, in a loud voice, to her companion, ''E's a prapper li'l whippersnapper id'n'e'!

CHAPTER NINETEEN

Schooldays & Childhood Memories

INK WELLS AND SKIPPING ROPES

In the 1930s, before moving to Paignton, I lived in Kingsteignton where I went to school. Before leaving home of a morning my mother would always pull my 'bloomer' legs down to full stretch 'to keep y' thighs warm', she'd say, at the same time tucking in a clean hankie above the elastic. At the first opportunity, under my pinafore, I deftly undid her handiwork!

At school, raps on knuckles with a wooden ruler were a daily occurrence. Our classroom sported a large easel with blackboard and a long T-square. Desks had lift-up surfaces and could seat six to eight children. Recesses for inkwells were spaced for two to share and written work always produced instant cries of, 'Miss, my nib's crossed,' or 'Please Miss, my inkwell's dry.' Skipping ropes, 'fag' cards, marbles, spinning tops and chewing on a 'ha'penny big argo bar' made journeys to school more bearable, as did the nature walks, affording sights and sounds of hovering skylarks, colourful flashes of flitting yellowhammers, linnets and goldfinches, and the harsh cries of jays mingled with the call of cuckoos in early spring.

THE YELLOW BRICK ROAD

A lot of what I value as a Paigntonian is stranded in my childhood and teens. Beyond the town dump, Clennon Valley was still a really rural corner of Torbay where nature had a lot of freedom to run riot. The low hill was once patched with cornfields and at the end of the summer I helped pitch the stoked sheaves onto the horse-drawn wagon. Across the valley Tanner's Lane (Road) and farmland still existed, now covered with houses. From there to the red steps below the prom at Goodrington North Sands was no distance at all and every summer kids from my neighbourhood gathered on the prom to swim off the steps at high tide. In the 1950s some of us with our girlfriends moved to the slope above in Cliff Gardens. Here we spread out our towels on the green lawn that looked down on Young's Park, the prom and the beach. In the immediate post-war years we congregated on the wide sandstone steps below and learned how to swim, the back-street way!

This was the era of hard cases like Ron Burridge and 'Beefy' Heath. What some of the 'ducklings', the small fry, endured would have horrified the toothless top dogs of today's nanny society. But we survived to watch the flash brigade diving off the prom railings into the sea, under Roundham Head. However, on the urban scene changes were in the air, because although the big swing bands continued to dominate the Saturday night dance hall, jazz clubs were gaining ground, in particular the places that offered 'trad', 'skiffle' and 'rock-n-roll'. The 'creep' sent the 'Teds' and their girls slowly and stiffly across the dance floor like creatures newly resurrected from the tombs of the pharaohs. On wet Saturday afternoons the flash of an usherette's torch would douse back-row passions in the Regent Cinema or Picture House! Outside in the world at large the Korean war mocked the claims made by politicians after Hiroshima that peace would reign forever, because it was thought a nuclear confrontation would mean the extinction of our species, but we still laughed and joked in the coffee bars.

DIRTY TRICKS!

School transport following the Second World War wasn't any better than it had ever been, in fact it was non-existent, excepting those lucky enough to have a bike or for older students attending the South Devon Technical College (then in Torquay), who used the train to Torre. In those days railway carriages were still based on the original stagecoach design, which meant each compartment was a complete unit (no corridor) and a door on either side of the coach, and a drop window operated by a leather strap. It so happened that one young fourteen-year-old lad, having just started his scholarship at the Technical College, was with a bunch of new friends all making for the train that would get them home to their various stations along the line to Brixham and Kingswear. It was pretty busy and one of the boys shouted from the end of the platform, 'There's an empty one down here!' whereupon the shy and unsuspecting lad dashed down the platform to the said carriage, jumping in just as the train pulled out, to discover to his horror he was in a carriage full of giggling girls, and as if that wasn't enough they had somehow managed to lock both doors of the compartment! The boy was trapped with no way out until the train pulled into Paignton station and the poor lad beat a hasty retreat headfirst through the carriage window, only to be confronted by an irate stationmaster yelling, 'What the hell do you think you're doing?'

BUTTERFLIES AND BEES

In early June 1939 my mother took me for a weekend on the moors. I wasn't too sure that I would like it; nevertheless I packed my little cardboard case and off we went on the bus from Paignton to Totnes where we took the train for Buckfastleigh. Quite a few people got on the train and we were lucky to find an empty carriage. At first I found the journey a wee bit boring, that is until we reached Staverton where the steam engine taking on water and the bustle of passengers getting on and off the train were quite fascinating. As the train pulled out of the station the scenery began to change. Suddenly we were deep in the Devonshire countryside: the variety of colourful flowers along the embankment was dazzling, rabbits ran alongside the train, birds flew in and out of the trees, butterflies and bees in their hundreds enjoyed what nature had to offer. The vista changed when the line joined the river and never shall I forget the feeling of tranquillity created by the deep-flowing Dart as it slowly made its way downstream. Fish jumped, dragonflies hovered and the water sparkled in the early morning sun, reaching up between the trees to highlight the different shapes and colours. The journey was like travelling through fairyland, simply magical, but ending all too soon when we reached Buckfastleigh station. Here the farmer was waiting with his Rover truck and drove us into the village of Scorrington, eventually pulling up outside a medieval thatched farmstead. We appeared to have arrived in the very heart of Devon. At the door to welcome us was his wife, a rotund lady with ruddy cheeks who ushered us into the farmhouse. She showed us to our room in which stood a huge iron bedstead, a washstand with a matching ensemble of a china washbasin, soap dish, water jug with hot water and clean towels ready for our use. 'When yur ready,' she said, 'come on down and I'll 'ave cup o' tea ready for 'e.'

We found our way to the lounge with its chintz-covered chairs and a blazing log fire in an old stone grate. 'A fire,' my mother gasped, somewhat surprised.

''T's cold evenings up yer early in t' season,' said the farmer's wife. 'Sit 'e down and I'll bring tray in.' We did as we were bid and very soon she returned with an enormous tray containing a steaming pot of tea, milk, sugar and freshly baked scones, a dish of home-made strawberry jam and thick yellow crusted clotted cream like we had never seen before. After tea we walked through country lanes and returned to the cottage ready for our evening meal, which consisted of roast pork, fresh farm vegetables, apple sauce and good thick gravy followed by a steamed pudding and, of course, more clotted cream. After supper we retired to the lounge and, following further cups of tea and lengthy chats with the farmer and his wife, we eventually retired to our room. The large iron-framed bed with its brass baubles had a wood casing base with coiled springs, overlaid with a deep feather mattress and crisp white linen, warmed by several stone hot water bottles. So old was the farmhouse that the seasoned oak floor had shrunk and twisted, dropping at least a foot on one side of the room, so we had to climb uphill to get into bed. We also got lost the next day and the farmer had to search for us. It was the most memorable weekend of my childhood.

CHASING DRAGONFLIES

A day trip to Spitchwick by the River Dart with the family in the 1930s was a summertime special for me and my cousin, always providing the car could make it to the top of the steepest hill on the moor, and only if everybody got out and pushed after the engine had cooled. Eventually we dropped down onto a green space called Holne Chase where, if we could find an opening through the bracken, we rolled the car gently towards the riverbank and there spent the day playing wild safari games, counting fish or chasing dragonflies in and out of the icy cold water. Numerous cups of tea were brewed on an open fire and delicious ham sandwiches and sticky buns were eaten. The uncles would disappear with fishing rods in hand, while the rest of the family played ball games on the green and Grandma sat in the shade of her umbrella, complaining of the heat, and all the time not a soul in sight.

Driving back to Paignton in the twilight of evening was an adventure in itself. On one occasion we got lost and found ourselves at the bottom of a remote farm lane among chickens and cows, having to wade knee-deep through mud and muck to ask a broad Devonian farmer, 'Where the devil are we?'

'Yo'd 'ave taken wrong turning at top of 'ill', he said and then proceeded in indescribable Devonian to explain the best way back, watching, as we departed, with a whimsical expression on his face. We could almost hear him mutter, 'them'll get lost again'!

A REAL ISLAND

Aunty and Uncle started to plan their forthcoming holiday with trips and meals out. 'Oh!' I said, listening to their conversation, 'I've never been in a hotel before.'

'Haven't you? Then we will treat you to lunch on Bigbury Island.'

We duly arrived and my heart thumped with excitement. I was going to a hotel on a real island. As we approached the tide was up so we had the additional pleasure of crossing the bar in the chain-drawn ferry, landing at Pilchard Inn, but this was not where we eventually had lunch, oh dear me no. We climbed the hill to the Bigbury Island Hotel, a grand Art Deco building facing the mainland. After a wash and tidy-up in the ladies 'Powder Room' we settled ourselves comfortably at one of the large circular tables in the huge airy dining room. Each table was immaculately laid with traditional crisp white damask tablecloths and matching napkins the size of afternoon tablecloths, elegant wine glasses and cutlery that sparkled like diamonds. Waiters moved silently around us as the menu was read and suggestions made about dishes I had never heard of. It was all so exciting. Suddenly Uncle stood up and announced, 'We are leaving.'

'Why? Whatever for?' I asked unbelievingly. Quickly gathering up our bits and pieces, he hustled us out of the hotel and back to the ferry.

'I was so looking forward to that,' I moaned.

'You shall still have lunch out,' said Uncle reassuringly and so we did; a ham salad, long faces and no further explanations at a tiny café back in Paignton.

PUNCH AND JUDY

As a five year old I loved sitting on Paignton beach among the huge crowd of children watching Mr Stafford's Punch and Judy show, mesmerised by the traditional knock-about of Judy hitting Punch for throwing the baby out, the antics of the crocodile, the hangman, the long string of sausages and Toby the dog. On one particular occasion while waiting for a performance to begin I was so excited with anticipation I wriggled my feet in the warm sand. Disaster! I cut my big toe on a broken bottle and missed the whole show!

CHAPTER TWENTY

A Mysterious Painting

THE OLD TANNERY

Frank Chubb was a slight, dapper little man. His thin features revealed a strong sensitivity and acute observation of the world about him, useful attributes for an up and coming artist. Frank moved into Paignton with his family following the First World War, after a nearby shell blast had damaged his hearing, making it difficult for him to communicate. Getting more and more depressed he visited his local doctor who recommended he should try painting. This doctor, on seeing one of his pictures, remarked, 'You've got a flair for this,' and encouraged him to keep it up.

According to his daughter he would often go out on a summer's evening to make sketches, noting changes in light and colour, before making a study of a painting he had in mind. He took a great interest in recording old buildings and one of his studies was a rare view of the island shops in Church Street (since demolished), as seen from the narrows in Winner Street (see page 47). As time passed Frank worked more and more in watercolours and eventually joined the Devon Arts Society. In 1969 he became a member of the newly formed Paignton Art and Crafts Society and was among their first members to exhibit several much-acclaimed watercolours alongside the well-known local painter and Royal Academy exhibitor John H. Willis, RBA, ARCA. Very soon Frank was being invited to submit paintings for the Britain in Watercolour Exhibition at the galleries of the Royal Watercolour Society in Conduit Street, London. Later, along with four others from the two local societies, he was invited to exhibit several paintings for the Summer Salon at the Royal Institute Galleries in Piccadilly. So far as is known, none of the works he submitted in London were photographed or recorded. Frank continued to paint prolifically. Many, if not most, of his paintings were of local subjects and can be seen in several homes around the Torbay area and beyond.

That he probably painted to commission is very likely, as there are several photographs taken of subjects hitherto unseen. One, a real mystery, is thought to be a piece of local history long since forgotten, a priceless record of what he notes on the reverse as 'The Old Tannery and Torbay'. But where was this tannery? Ask as one may, nobody seems to know and most say it never existed. Place names can sometimes give a clue as to what might have been going on in a particular area in the past, so perhaps Tanners Road, also known as Tanners

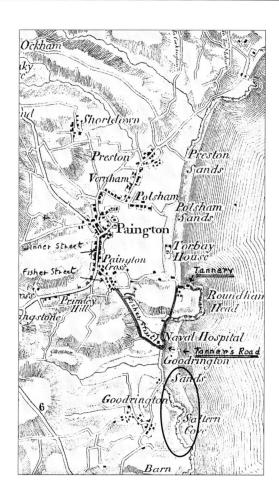

Circled on the map is the road from Brixham to Paignton as it used to be. (*Peggy Parnell*)

Lane, which once led off the Brixham to Paignton road towards Goodrington House and the old naval hospital on Goodrington beach, might suggest a tannery was somewhere nearby. But does Tanners Road really signify a tanning industry was here and is it a coincidence that a Mr George Tanner, a newcomer to Paignton in the early 1880s, moved into Goodrington House (the old guard house) following the closure of the naval hospital in about 1816. In the past a man's name indicated his work or trade, so did Mr Tanner have connections with this tannery business? A Paignton map of 1809 (still in use in 1817) shows that the original road/trackway from Brixham to Paignton actually led straight into the hospital, and what we have come to know as Tanners Road (Tanners Lane by 1888) was already in existence and formed part of Fisher Street, which eventually became part of Dartmouth Road. Is this map telling us something? Another possible lead in connection with this industry is a reference in the *Paignton Observer* of 1854 to a Higher and Lower Tanners Down, and Billings' Directory of 1857 also lists, among the various residents of Goodrington Sands, a shoemaker named Nicholas Langdon.

The Old Tannery and Torbay, by Frank Chubb. (*Peggy Parnell*)

Frank's painting shows a collection of strange buildings that appear to be sited on a small headland. Is it possible that he was using artist's licence and his painting was of a place that looked something like Torbay, or did he actually set up his easel somewhere along the Torbay coastline a short distance from his chosen subject? If so his painting suggests that he was looking towards Torquay and the only likely place this could be was on an outcrop called Paignton Head above Fairy Cove. Given the artist's observation of the scenery he saw, he could not have been any further round the coast than on Roundham Head as the perspective would not have correlated with his rendering of the subject, which indicates a distant land mass remarkably like that of Torquay. The date of this painting must have been somewhere about the late 1920s to early 1930s, which fits nicely with the Paignton Urban District Council's development of Young's Park in 1921, when various properties were being purchased for future demolition. No doubt Frank, with his eye to painting old buildings, would have been quickly on the spot to record this interesting miscellany of buildings perched perilously on the edge of Paignton Head before they were demolished.

Paignton Head, most likely the site of the tannery. (*Peggy Parnell*)

At this time both Paignton Head and Roundham Head extended several feet further out towards the sea, with a path and a wooden bridge spanning the small inlet of Savage Hole that linked the two headlands. Both bridge and path have long since disappeared; even so, a recent photograph is extremely interesting, given the years of coastal erosion, as it shows the alignment of Paignton Head is remarkably like Frank's painting.

Above Fairy Cove there were a considerable number of old sandstone foundations still visible in the 1940s and '50s, in particular one or two buildings that might have been the sixteenth-century storehouses mentioned in the Pembroke Survey but could equally have been connected with the old tannery. But the mystery deepens for there is not a single map, old or new, that indicates any tannery anywhere in or near Paignton, let alone on Paignton Head, but with the number of boot-making shops and saddlers around in the early nineteenth century one surely must have existed.

Interestingly an 1840 map of Paignton shows a steep track leading from an old farm that once existed at its base on the Goodrington side. This track is still in existence and leads straight across Roundham Head to 'Le Key' (the harbour). Over the years this path has been known by various names, such as Breakneck Hill and Lovers Lane. In addition to this, in an old guidebook map of 1900 can be seen a short lane leading out from the harbour towards Paignton Head where a small dot might suggest an area where the tannery could have been. However, both the tannery and Breakneck Hill existed long before the rock walk was built in 1931. The old farm, known as Goodrington Cottage, sat on the edge of a marsh nearby a large pool fed by a freshwater stream and was called Mazepool by an earlier generation of Paigntonians (1850s), later May's Pool; it eventually became the Goodrington Boating Lake. This farm was for a time owned by the Misses Brown and run as tea-rooms and guesthouse until the PUDC bought both it and the marshes, finally demolishing the building and its outhouses in 1928.

There used to be an old story about Mazepool and its 'fathomless bottom', which, when the area was being developed, was discovered to be only 2ft deep. Was this perhaps a story told by the tanners to keep people away. Tanneries were always placed near a stream or river and, if as thought, the industry was situated on the hill above this could well have been the reason. Indeed the actual tannery

May's Pool (once known as Mazepool). (*Roy Authors*)

was well placed high above the sea, probably for the quick disposal of waste materials. In those days there were no blue flags! Is it just possible a well-known local ghost legend got entwined with the tanners' deep pool tale and was used by smugglers to cover up their illegal activities in the years between 1700 and 1860?

A stroll around Fairy Cove today reveals how much of the coastline has been eaten away by the sea. Gone is an old sandstone building that was in days gone by approached by a steep rock climb, where many young lovers may have experienced their first kiss and certainly where one in particular jibbed at being enticed into its stinking interior, damp and riddled with untold creepy-crawlies, by a 1939 evacuee boyfriend! Whatever buildings remain in this area, all are of historical interest.

Most towns would have had a tannery and, already mentioned, Paignton did have a considerable number of shoe and leather shops between 1799 and 1899. So the evidence weighs in favour of a tannery existing somewhere on the outskirts of this ancient town, with the strong possibility that it was on Paignton Head overlooking Torbay, as Frank Chubb recorded. There is absolutely no reason why Frank should have painted this site if it didn't exist. But at the time of writing it remains an enigma that not one map, nor one book or one person records these buildings, which the painting reveals once stood on Paignton Head above Fairy Cove. It is as though the new tourist town of Paignton would not admit to having a tannery on its shoreline.

CHAPTER TWENTY-ONE

The War Years

NOT A TRUE DEVONIAN

My first sight of Paignton was before the Second World War when, as a schoolboy during the summer holidays, my parents and I stayed at the Tembani Hotel, Preston, with Mr and Mrs Christmas in charge. I recall coach tours around the area in Grey Cars, fishing trips in a small dinghy hired from Mr Bradshaw at Paignton harbour, occasional visits to the concert party in the Adelphi Theatre, cricket at Queens Park and the last days of balmy peace!

The entrance to Adelphi Gardens. (*Peggy Parnell*)

The exterior of Deller's Café. This beautiful building was demolished in 1965. (*T. Moss*)

In the summer of 1939 my parents rented a furnished house opposite the Redcliffe Hotel. One of my last and lasting memories of peacetime was late on Friday evening, 1 September, listening to the hotel dance band with Rex Sercombe playing 'Down Mexico Way', 'Deep Purple' and 'The Last Waltz'. Back home in Sussex on the following Sunday, like millions of others, we heard the declaration of war.

Although not a true Devonian I do claim county status by residential qualification, for in May or June 1940 we moved permanently to Paignton. My first wartime memory was the Dunkirk evacuation and seeing part of the East Kent Regiment (The Buffs) regrouping on Paignton seafront.

Anyone who lived in Paignton during the mid-1940s will have his or her own memory of Deller's Café. I particularly recall school holidays when a gang of between six and twelve of us youngsters used to congregate in the café (then managed by Frank Craze) for morning coffee, the main attraction being the three-piece band led by pianist Vic Hocking. Occupying a corner of the restaurant next to the band we regularly demanded musical requests. What a nuisance we must have been to other customers!

Between holidays, schooling had to be faced – Mr Motts Academy in Primley Park, School Certificate (taken at Dartington Hall) and another 'crammer' at Torquay. By this time military service was looming, but first I joined the Home Guard, known as 'Dad's Army', and went into the local Signals platoon.

Training and practice in Morse code and semaphore was under the guidance of Mr Emanuel Beare (Emanuel Beare's department store, Victoria Street) and true to Dad's Army form he was almost deaf with very bad eyesight – ideal for transmission of messages by sound and flag!

After a short stint teaching at Montpelier School I volunteered for a Service Engineering course at Newport, but when home on a short leave one day found my return coincided with the D-Day embarkation. Because of the high security surrounding this operation, I had to get a special pass to enter Torbay. On these few days at home in Tweenaway I witnessed the many columns of transport carrying mostly American troops and equipment, lining up for the embarkation. After the war I returned to Paignton, married Anita Hughes, started in business and began the process of becoming a Devonian. (John Wright, auctioneer and house agent, Paignton 1950–80)

GOOD OLD DB'N

Like many local boys in the First World War, Michael Adams was called up at the start of the Second World War and soon after found himself in France where he was lucky to escape alive during the battle of Dunkirk. For a while he served in Italy, but it was when he found himself along with 25,000 lads from the West Country en route to Egypt that his memories are most vivid. Michael explained how hundreds of chaps were picked up from Gloucester, and elaborates:

> We were an enormous number of men and we all knew we were going to a hot climate on finding mammoth sun hats in our kits, so guessed it was probably Egypt. Dead secret of course! We sailed out on 1 June, a beautiful hot summer's day. Two days later it was snowing! We thought, Egypt? There seemed to be hundreds of ships and we were all sailing together up around Iceland, Greenland and down the coast of America, never touching land. A hot climate! Something peculiar was going on. Apparently the ships were deviating around the north Atlantic to avoid the German U-boats and when we reached a certain spot the fleet belted across the Atlantic to Africa. Eventually the convoy pulled into Freetown for refuelling then continued around the Cape and up into the Red Sea to Tripoli.

On arrival everybody went down with dysentery. Michael got it badly and was in hospital for three weeks; so weak he had to be carried on a stretcher into the recovery marquee. Here he was placed on a bed near the tent flaps. There was no lighting and Michael remembered saying to the orderly, 'Don't forget I'm in here.' They were well catered for with their own mess and everything necessary. Then one evening as Michael lay on his bed listening to the piped radio in the background with Deanna Durbin singing 'Home Sweet Home' he burst into tears. All he wanted was to go home. Suddenly a breeze lifted the tent flap and he saw a wonderful velvet sky with stars like lanterns, a truly remarkable sight, one he'd never seen the like of before.

Those who were stronger were allowed to go on little trips to the NAAFI or the cinema. On one particular occasion several guys were late back and with no lights they scrambled into bed the best they could. Someone was settling into the bed next to Michael and to his surprise was talking away in broad Devonian. When it was all quiet Michael asked, 'What part of Devon do you come from?'

'Oh!' came a sharp retort. 'Didn't know t'were anybody in there. Why? Are you Db'n?'

'Yes,' replied Michael.

The voice continued, 'I'm from 'arbertonford, where's you from?'

'I'm from Pnt'n.'

'Pnt'n?', the chap repeated, 'Oh! I knows Pnt'n. I drives a cattle truck and takes Mr Williams' bullocks from the station to the slaughter yard under the arch in Church Street, t'em also 'as a stable there.'

'Yes, I know, my father stands his pony there.'

'It beain't that there little bugger, the black 'un, is it?'

'Actually it's a stallion and he's a joy to handle. My father bought him for £1 off some gypsies who'd whipped her off Dartmoor.'

'You've got a little dog too 'avent 'e, called Soda?'

'Yep! Two: Whisky and Soda.'

And so the conversation continued well into the early hours. Can you imagine in the middle of the night thousands of miles away, two lonely soldiers talking about home? It was simply wonderful.

As a lad Michael had worked for a time in his father's workshop, next to Barns House in Colley End, using Dad's black stallion and cart for deliveries, the same pony he talked about in Egypt. (Extract from Michael Adams' *Memoirs*, 2002)

HOW KITCHENS WERE

Eating out during the Second Word War was very difficult, there being only one or two restaurants, so to make sure that people in towns throughout England got a good nourishing meal the government organised the British Restaurants. The parents of a young fifteen-year-old Paignton girl just starting at a Secretarial College in Torquay were concerned that this type of eating-house was not suitable for her. Apart from anything else they considered she wouldn't get an adequate meal, so arranged for her to have lunch with their friends in nearby Bampfield Road. The young girl had not visited the house since she was a tiny tot and was amazed to discover a Victorian kitchen and across the room, sitting beside a well-polished blackened kitchen range upon which was a prattling kettle beside numerous pots of boiling carrots, cabbage, dumplings, 'Ma' Treed wrapped in a print apron, her white hair pulled back into a bun at the nape of her neck and grasping a long iron poker, with which she periodically poked the fire while piling on fresh coal and wood. At intervals she opened the heavy oven door and pulled forth a huge tray of sizzling potatoes surrounding an enormous joint (her husband was a butcher!) simply oozing in hot dripping. She reached for a large iron spoon and basted the contents before returning them to the oven. She regularly checked the iron saucepans with their boiling vegetables and stirred the huge pot of soup. Hanging from the ceiling were herbs, dried fish, pheasants and all manner of things drying. Beneath it, in the middle of the room, was a massive well-scrubbed wooden table where the daughter of the house was busily laying huge steel cutlery for the family meal. The warmth and smells in this strange kitchen on a cold winter's day were wonderful and so was the meal!

GREAT FUN WAS HAD

During the early days of the Second World War I decided my real ambition was to be an accountant so my dad, who knew a practising accountant, asked his advice as to whether my education at the Torquay Technical College was sufficient to enter the profession, He said there was no way I would be able to pursue this without a school-leaving certificate. As it turned out I left college early!

When the principal of the college learnt that I was looking for a job, he told me about a vacancy for a junior clerk at the Torquay Corporation, I duly applied and was granted an interview, but my mother insisted on accompanying me and even came into the Deputy Borough Engineer's office with me. That so embarrassed me I very nearly walked out; however, I did get the job, which was in the Highways Depot at St Marychurch. Because my mother and Mr Foale, who conducted the interview, knew one another through business, I was called David, whereas most of my colleagues were known by their surnames. Needless to say it took a long time to be accepted by the staff!

I took over from a girl called Molly who had been called up to work in the Fire Service. Molly would leave off doing her work while chatting up all the fellows who came into the office and my first job was to draw a line in the 'signing-in book' at 9am, which meant anyone under that line was late. Molly, who was always late, made sure she signed in before the line was drawn, which meant she along with everyone else was on time. I don't know how she managed when she joined the Fire Service.

Before Molly left she did manage to teach me how to work the telephone and switchboard, but within a month she was gone and I found myself having to continue her work. My first job as junior office boy was to reorganise the filing of delivery notes. Unfortunately not a soul told me what was required and in my wisdom I put all the delivery notes from firms with 'The' in their title under 'T' and any with Messrs under 'M', – in those days the majority of firms had this on their headings. Great fun was had by all on discovering the 'T' and 'M' files were full to capacity, resulting in no one finding anything! After being told off good and proper I started again and this time got it right. Mind you, I still hate filing!

A PAIGNTONIAN FROM KENT

An elderly lady, now living in Paignton, can vividly recall voices from the past of her hometown in Maidstone, Kent. It was 15 September 1940 and the Battle of Britain had just begun. A party of guests were invited for tea, so her mother's precious food store was raided and the best tea service was laid out in the dining room. But everyone was on the lawn with its open views across the town and

North Downs, excitedly watching the dog fights in the sky with cheer upon cheer when an enemy plane was hit, and shocked silence when it was one of ours. Mother shouted, 'Tea is brewed!' but all requests to come to the table were ignored, so she served tea in the garden with severe warnings that it was her best tea service! That evening, while they were singing around the piano, the town was subjected to an air attack that lasted the whole weekend, and all began to realise just how much they and the nation owed to those dog fights in the sky. Only two of that garden party are still alive today, but the tea service remains complete and undamaged.

TIME MOVED ON

During the First World War Station Square was cordoned off to allow wounded soldiers access to the ambulances waiting to transport them to Oldway, then a convalescent hospital. A small girl of about eight years watched the proceedings from her drawing room window. Many years later, in 1932, her father sold their house, and following its demolition the Regent Cinema appeared (now Regent House). In time the family moved on. Then came the Second World War and the same little girl, now grown up, joined the Women's Land Army. On one occasion her group, together with a contingent from Exeter, was detailed to blitz the Clennon Valley refuse tip. They did and killed over 500 rats!

Patients in Oldway Hospital enjoying Christmas during the First World War. (*Peggy Parnell*)

THE REAL DAD'S ARMY

Two boys living in Church Street had a rather spoilt overfed cat with a fine tail which rarely left the house. One day one of the lads decided it should have an outing and took the cat across the road to his friend in the shop opposite. The cat struggled, managed to escape and shot out across the road. At that precise moment a detachment of soldiers came marching down Church Street towards Hyde Road. In its eagerness to get away the cat cut straight through the platoon, tripping up one soldier after another in its wake, and in a matter of seconds the whole platoon was in chaos. The NCO called the platoon to a halt and realigned them, by which time the cat, having done its worst, was nowhere to be seen!

NUNS FIGHTING FURIOUSLY

One night in January 1942 over 400 incendiaries fell on the town. One of the wardens on duty in Ebenezer Road was dealing with the small but lethal bombs when one exploded and killed him. On the same night a number of bombs landed on the roof of the Marist Convent (now Tower House School), where the nuns fought furiously to extinguish them. The bombs also destroyed part of the convent's garden wall. Incendiary bombs were not only designed to burn and explode, but also to illuminate an area so that the German bombers could pick out any defences they thought a town might have – in this case Torbay.

Paignton's 'G' group of ARP (Air Raid Precaution) wardens during the Second World War ready with stirrup pump, shovel, lantern, warning bell, first-aid box and buckets of sand for quenching incendiary bombs. (Herald & Express, *1959*)

An Innocent Lad!

During the Second World War teenage lads often claimed to be older than they were in order to join up. One particular young rating did just that and very soon found himself in the position of having to run errands for his senior officers. A sort of pass-the-parcel situation arose, the parcel in question containing NAAFI food, which he very soon discovered could lead a naive lad into severely hot water. Fortunately for him the top brass was one of the parcel receivers, so when confronted at the inquiry with his innocent misdeeds he just happened to mention this fact. Mildly blackmailing the senior officer, he remarked, 'I'll say no more if my papers remain unmarked.' His reports did remain clean, but the petty officer that made the charge kept an accusing eye on him. Come demob day, on passing through with his civvy clothes in hand, the lad nonchalantly remarked to this officer, 'Be careful where you walk around Plymouth or you may have an accident!'

A Lucky Dog

During the Second World War a soldier helping save people during a severe London raid heard some whimpering among the ruins of a freshly bombed building. Pulling the timbers and masonry apart he discovered a little dog covered in dust and very much alive. He gave him some water and later a piece of his sandwich, after which the dog followed him everywhere. Days later the soldier boarded a GWR train at Paddington for duty in the south west. Having arranged his gear he sat down in the only available carriage, and as the train pulled away began to take in his environment, only to discover the liver-and-white spaniel was still at his side. Eventually the train pulled into Furzeham station, Brixham. Patting the dog he said, 'You're a nice old thing, but this is the end of the journey for you, I'm afraid doggies are not allowed in the barracks.' On alighting from the train the soldier got talking to a local fire officer and asked him if he could find the poor animal a home. The fire officer looked down at the pleading brown eyes and decided he just couldn't refuse him, even though with rationing there was little hope of finding him a home, but he would take him back for the night in the hope that he could find someone. Days passed into months the months into years, during which time the dog became known to the fire officer and his family as Major, after the soldier who had saved his life in that horrific blitz.

A Silver Cigarette Case

Early in January 1917 I made my appearance into the world at the South Eden nursing home, now the Esplanade Hotel. My education started in Winner Street at Melbourne School (presently Crofts Garage) where, as far as I can remember, Miss Hart was the headmistress. At the age of nine my father decided to enrol me as a pupil in a local private school, but class distinction was very much a ruling factor and as he was not a professional man I was, needless to say, turned down. So instead I went as a boarder to Caterham School in Surrey where I remained for just over six years – apart from the usual holidays of course. On leaving this school I returned home, and to further my education attended a small, I suppose one could say a finishing school, run by Mr Motts, a well-known and highly qualified tutor who started a small school in his front room at Conway Road where, as far as I remember, there were never more than six pupils at a time.

After leaving Mr Motts I worked for several jewellers and finally secured a job with Asprey's in London where I had the opportunity to study gemmology at the London Polytechnic. Working at Asprey's – one of the top jewellers in Bond Street – gave me the opportunity to see many famous people of the day. One of their customers was Hailie Selassie, Emperor of Ethiopia, who escaped to England in 1938/9 and lived in Browns Hotel, situated just behind Asprey's. Tragically at the end of the war he returned to his country and was assassinated. When Prime Minister Chamberlain returned from Munich on 28 September 1938, waving his piece of paper with the words 'Peace in our Time', the incident clearly inspired a particularly wealthy gentleman to order from Asprey's a silver cigarette case engraved on the front with a map of Europe inlaid in gold, showing the route Chamberlain had taken. When it was finished I took it to 10 Downing Street by taxi, with clear instructions that it should be given to the Prime Minister himself. I never thought a young Paignton boy would set foot in No. 10.

On leaving Asprey's in September 1939 I decided to join the Royal Air Force for the duration of the war, and like thousands of others was sent to Padgate to toughen up for service life. At one particular parade the sergeant shouted, 'Ricks, I'll send you a bloody postcard when I want you to present arms!' The trouble was that the obsolete First World War rifles were so heavy to lift that I, being only a little fellow, was often a second or two behind the rest of the squad lifting it onto my shoulder.

One day an unexpected forty-eight hour pass decided me to go home so I caught a train to Paignton. Thoroughly exhausted, I fell asleep and consequently failed to change trains at Newton Abbot. Waking up at Totnes station late in the night, I discovered to my horror that transport to Paignton was unavailable, so decided to walk home and was almost arrested climbing over our back gate in the early hours of the morning!

Nevertheless I managed to complete six and a half years in the RAF and in the end my survival was down to an unknown WAAF to whom I owe my grateful thanks for carefully packing my parachute, which later saved my life.

A PLATE OR TWO OF CAKES

Immediately following Dunkirk army camps started to appear in the fields around Paignton and many local people got involved in various projects to help make life a little more pleasant for the soldiers, most of whom were only young lads. It so happened that two ladies who lived on Kings Ash Hill had a garden that adjoined one of these camps, and possibly because of their proximity to the camp at the rear of their house they found themselves billeting a NAAFI officer. These ladies loved cooking and soon found themselves entertaining the officer and a few of his comrades with cups of tea and a plate or two of freshly baked cakes. The soldiers were so delighted with their cooking abilities that it was eventually suggested that they might like to set up a canteen between the camp and their back garden. The two ladies, Edie and Maudie, were only too pleased to do this as their part in the war effort and in no time at all a wooden dais was erected over the hedge. Indeed it was a proper shop complete with a roof against rain and sun, and became known as the 'Table Under the Hedge'. The lads were delighted with such a handy source of excellent home baking along with a cuppa and a friendly chat, both of which the two ladies kept up a continuous supply.

Towards the end of the war the British soldiers moved on and the American army moved in, taking over the camps vacated by the British Army, which included the one behind Edie and Maudie's house. Soon the American soldiers discovered their 'Table Under the Hedge' and, like the English boys, were delighted with such a friendly corner complete with a wonderful supply of home cookies next to their camp. Excepting the day when Edie and Maudie asked if everything was to their liking and one of the officers remarked, 'Well ma'am, your canteen is sure great, but please would it be possible to have coffee instead of tea?' Another officer remarked, 'Your donuts are real good, but do you have proper donuts with a hole?'

'A donut with a hole?' the ladies gasped.

'Yes', came the reply. 'That's the way we have them back home. Say, ma'am, would you like us to show you how to make them?' In no time at all the camp chef was giving them instructions and even supplied some of the necessary ingredients, and thus followed yet another production line of cakes: donuts with a hole.

The canteen continued to flourish, with Edie and Maudie searching every available food store for whatever foods they could find. The wonderful business of home cookies and a friendly chat lasted until the early hours of D-Day, 6 June 1944, and all the guys – as the American referred to themselves – disappeared as if by magic, leaving every camp empty.

NOT PERMITTED

During the Second World War it was not permitted for ice cream to be made or sold throughout the British Isles. When the American soldiers arrived in Paignton they discovered, to their utter dismay, no ice cream! They very soon demanded something be done about this and in consequence Pelosi's ice-cream parlour, one of the leading ice-cream makers in Paignton, if not Torbay, was ordered to pull out of storage all its ice-cream making equipment. Not only vanilla was requested, but many other flavours which the lads were used to having back home in the USA, for example chocolate – almost forgotten in England – strawberry, raspberry and an exotic fruit called pineapple, all of which were unobtainable in England. So that the Americans could continue having what they were accustomed to at home, the American Army supplied the ingredients required, but still had to find a 10-gallon milk supply to set up the machines for each mix. Needless to say milk was rationed in England, so a special licence was needed to obtain such a huge quantity, even though it was a farming area. Officially the people of Paignton did not get one taste of these succulent flavoured ice-creams, but, just occasionally, some found their way into the mouths of a few lucky people. It was certainly a question of not what you knew, but whom you knew!

RISQUÉ READING

The Americans had a very good supply of American magazines, which were duly disposed of in the camp trash bins and later collected by the local authority refuse collectors. These rare magazines managed to find their way into the hands of many local residents, who were starved of such juicy reading! One young man was extremely frustrated when he discovered the most interesting pages of his salvaged magazine were missing!

CHAPTER TWENTY-TWO

When It Was Over

IN TRUE DICKENSIAN FASHION

Like his father before him after the First World War, Michael Adams didn't marry until the war had ended, and when he did he found the post-war period very difficult with all the shortages. However, he luckily discovered a young furnisher named Frank Martin, who had just started a business in Winner Street. Apparently this trader's father was a dealer in furniture and owned a warehouse. Frank's boyhood had been very unhappy, indeed so bad that by the time he was a teenager he decided he had had enough and left home. Eventually he became a member of the local Methodist church and found them a great help. Having

Frank waiting for his next customer. (*Herald & Express*)

managed to save a little money and with their guidance he rented a shop next to Evans the baker on the corner of New Street, stocking it with furnishings from a well-known firm called Lebus. Ever enterprising, he hired the public hall-cum-theatre (today the Palace Theatre) for a week's grand sale, allowing his customers two weeks in which to pay, and was very soon selling ahead of his stock. But poor Frank, with nowhere to live, in true Dickensian fashion slept under the counter!

Michael recalled vividly those drab post-war days, the problems with coupons and the awful shortages, and in particular his discovery that there was no such thing as fitted carpets, only squares, the largest being about 12ft x 9ft. Eventually he and his wife visited Frank's shop to see what he had in the way of floor covering. Looking through the different rolls of carpet and grumbling about the size, Michael eventually pulled one out and dumped it on the floor saying, 'That'll suit me.'

Frank Martin gasped, 'That's bigger than the place I live in!' (Extract from Michael Adams' *Memoirs*, 2002)

HE WHO EXPECTS

During and after the First World War, among many valuable trading commodities on the black market were petrol coupons. A local dairyman had a customer who bragged he could obtain a quantity of petrol coupons, so the dairyman allowed him more than his ration of bacon, in return for which he was promised a quantity of coupons. Later that evening in the pub the dairyman kept plying his customer with beer in anticipation of a goodly handout. When eventually the customer was approached he replied, 'Oh! Of course', and thrusting his hand into his pocket put a fist full of coupons into the dairyman's palm who, needless to say, was delighted until he opened his hand. Shrieking an unholy oath, he yelped, 'only two measly gallons after all the beer I've bought the miserable bastard'. One week later petrol rationing ceased!

And still the dairyman had not learnt his lesson! A retired farmer, who had bought little in the way of clothes during the war, collected a lot of clothing coupons and again in the pub generously passed them to his friend. Next day clothes rationing came to an end!

A CULTURE SHOCK

Shortly after my mother and stepfather married in 1949 they moved into an old farm worker's cottage at Weekaborough near Marldon. Coming from Paignton where she had on-tap water, electricity and indoor sanitation, it was something of a culture shock for my mother to discover her new home was in the middle of a field, and the only water supply was an old iron pump outside the house, shared by the neighbours next door. But that was not all. She then found the only sanitation was a 'bog hole' some distance from the house covered by a small wooden shed, which had a seat (of well-rotted wood) with a hole straight into the ground. On a nail nearby a supply of carefully cut newspaper, threaded onto string, sufficed for the most necessary of needs. Other than that it was a good old 'chamber pot' in the bedroom, named by me 'Charlie-goes-under'. As if this wasn't enough there was no sink indoors, so washing was done in a basin and the water emptied into a bucket. On washday, clothes were soaked in a wooden trough outside. Frosty weather was good as it helped to whiten the sheets. Mother had to do all her cooking, including a full roast dinner on Sundays, on a small oil-fired cooker. However, the larder, large enough to walk into, faced north with a slab of slate for keeping butter and cream cool in warm weather. In the winter the house was heated from an old stone fireplace fuelled by huge logs obtained from the farm – the scent of beech wood burning is something I shall always remember. That lovely old fireplace certainly did a good job keeping the house warm and a kettle boiling all day. Glowing embers would survive to the following morning, from which mother would set up another fire. To have a bath was a major feat, which meant taking down the old galvanised bath that hung in one of the sheds outside and then waiting for kettles and pans of water to heat up. The thought of my rather large stepfather trying to get into that coffin-shaped bath was mind-boggling to say the least.

One civilised aspect of going to stay with my mother and stepfather was that Sam had a motorbike and sidecar and would drive up from Weekaborough to the main Newton to Totnes road and meet me at the bus stop. It was always great fun driving across the farmland with its deep furrows, scattering crows and seagulls in all directions – but not so funny listening to the mice scratching in the roof and behind the walls of my bedroom all night!

THE MONKEY POLE

On the headland above Saltern Cove used to be what many Paigntonians called a monkey-pole. Some say it was an ordnance lookout post, but in actual fact it was for firing rockets out to sea to warn ships that came in too close to the shore and also for hauling stranded people up from the rocks below. To the many lovers it was an ideal place to engrave their initials for posterity, which included mine and my boyfriend who, forty years on, became my second husband. This post with its many signatures much overwritten can still be seen, but now on Berry Head.

Sea rescue equipment. (*Peggy Parnell*)

LIKE ICING ON THE CAKE

Cold weather is almost unheard of in Torbay, so the winter of 1947 was one of the most extraordinary on record. Snow lay around for weeks on end and the sea froze as it washed the coastal walls, making the rough sandstone walls look like sugar icing on a cake. Everything froze in the wake of severe fuel shortages, and the only warmth one newlywed couple had in their two rented rooms was from what they could burn in an old Victorian grate. With constant electricity cuts and only a few candles, finding light in the long dark winter evenings was a problem for most people, but this young couple, thanks to their Gran's foresight, were well stocked up with a large bundle of candles, a leftover from the Second World War. Luckily the blackened wrought-iron fire grate had two swing hobs upon which could be boiled a kettle and a small saucepan for soup. So blessed, they passed many a cosy evening supping soup and cups of a well-known drink called Camp Coffee. They made toast lashed with dripping collected from their meagre ration of meat, eaten with relish in the glow of a small but warming fire, while listening on a crackly radio to such *Children's Hour* favourites as *Toy Town* and on Sundays *The Jewels of the Madonna*, based on the opera by Wolf-Ferrari.

A DAY TO REMEMBER

On 2 June 1953, on their own with five children between them and no money, two young mums wondered what they could do for Queen Elizabeth II's coronation. Eventually they decided something must be done on this royal day, if only for the children's sake. So clutching a souvenir programme each they spent the morning sitting around a small radio, dressed in red, white and blue, listening to the ceremony with a small feast ready to hand. They described each stage of the procession to the children who sat enchanted at the procession of a fairytale golden coach with its beautiful princess, when suddenly a little voice chirped, 'Is it real?' With the procession over they all walked down to the promenade in their best summer clothes where they danced to the music of Charles Shadwell's band until (would you believe in June?) flakes of snow drove them home for hot drinks and warm clothing. Come the evening, suitably dressed in winter coats, they returned to watch the grand firework display. At the end of the day, after the two families returned to their respective homes and the children had fallen exhausted into their respective beds, the mums agreed it had certainly been a day to remember.

CHAPTER TWENTY-THREE

Entertainment

GOING TO THE FLICKS

Many a happy afternoon was spent visiting the cinemas in Torbay, but the one I enjoyed the most was the cosy little Paignton Picture House, known in its early day as Deller's Picture House; so called because Mr Deller, a local business entrepreneur and owner of the new Deller's Café, also invested significantly in the development of this, one of the earliest purpose-built cinemas in England, if not Europe.

In about 1909 this little cinema started its life in a hotel called The Broadmead next to the station, where under canvas at the rear of the building an effort to show 'moving pictures' for the first time was being made. These moving pictures were a terrific novelty when first shown in England in the late 1890s, but by 1909 considerable advancement had been made. Far-seeing local business people like Mr Dellar began to see a potential in the 'Bioscope' that had already become very popular entertainment with Hancock's travelling fairs here in the south west. These were especially appreciated as they preceded their shows with a troop of delectable dancing girls clad in pink tights, a delight to the local young men. So plans were laid and construction started to transform this hotel into a luxury picture palace, but like so many expensive projects the building was held back because of financial problems. Not to be beaten, Mr Deller along with several likeminded business men of Paignton purchased the Broadmead Hotel, and built a hall onto the back where people could see the moving pictures in greater comfort.

By 1910 the bioscope had advanced considerably and the very first news reports, albeit extremely limited pictures of the South African Boer War lasting only a few minutes, were shown. As part of this wonderful phenomenon a pianist and coloured slides were put on to keep the audience entertained between the flickering exposures, and particularly when the equipment broke down! One year later new plans for a grand purpose-built cinematography house on the Broadmead Hotel site were once again being considered. The hotel, being conveniently situated next to the station, was an ideal distribution centre for the other picture houses that would soon follow, so from the start it was designed to take in and distribute all the latest films. It was intended to be a classy building (in the style of the old music hall theatres) in order to attract the many distinguished people from across a wide area, whereas up the town opposite the old Town Hall, the new Electric Cinema appealed mainly to the earthy (agricultural) populace of Paignton. However, according to the records of Denis Bond (descendant of Leisure 2000, Torbay Road) Paignton's Picture House was continually besieged with money problems. These dogged the whole course of construction and consequently the Picture House was built several square feet smaller than originally intended. Nevertheless in about 1912 the Broadmead Hotel was demolished, which cost around £10, and the grand façade of Torbay's first purpose-built cinema began to appear. When the doors officially opened in 1913, its first silent movie was *Tilly's Lost Romance*, produced by Essery Productions, classified as a comedy farce, produced by Essery Productions together with a Gaumont Newsreel. This was followed by such classics as the Charlie Chaplin films, popular for many years. The following year came newsreels of the First World War. The earliest silent movies were accompanied by a pianist to emphasise the story, but because the cinema was perceived as a theatre with all its traditional comforts and music hall entertainments, the management would put on various forms of entertainment during the intervals.

So the first patrons of the new purpose-built cinema would have walked into a cosy theatre lavishly decorated in true theatrical style with a grand tympanum over the proscenium arch, and plush burgundy red tabs (curtains) gracing the white screen. Settling comfortably into the scallop-backed red plush seating, patrons listened to music played by the cinema's own twenty-one-piece orchestra situated in a fine orchestra pit with shining brass rails and matching burgundy drapes. This orchestra not only entertained cinema patrons, they also assisted the pianist with mood music backing. Mr Lambshead who promoted the orchestra

Interior of one of the oldest purpose-built cinemas known. (*Herald & Express*)

The Americans parking their jeep outside the Torbay Cinema (the Paignton Picture House). (*Frank Pearce*, The Book of Paignton, *Halsgrove, 2001*)

also had an arrangement whereby three or four of his instumentalists could play in Mr Deller's café along the road. The pit had a special room at the side for stacking the great quantity of music sheets that were regularly used, and eventually there were two grand pianos, the second acquired by the management from Paris Singer who became one of the cinema's regular patrons. So, as originally envisaged, this cinema was indeed a classy theatre designed to attract the right sort of people; it was named the Paignton Picture House.

The first manager was a Mr Fred Bunting, and the first violinist was a Mr Clifford Rainbow, who on one occasion complained bitterly to Fred Bunting that the projectionist was turning the film so fast that the orchestra was threatening to walk out. Apparently the projectionist got so excited by the film that he was totally unaware that he was turning the handle faster and faster!

The 1920s was the period when my aunt spent as much time as possible in the back row with my uncle watching these silent movies, and sometimes, if they could afford it, in one of the three boxes of this elegant cinema, one of which was boarded off when new fire precautions came in. It was here such notable dignitaries as Paris Singer with Isadora Duncan and Edgar Wallace sat watching such films as *The Train Robbers*, yelling and shouting along with everyone else. Agatha Christie also enjoyed visiting this little cinema and would arrive with her chauffeur who always sat with her and made sure that she had a blanket over her knees. In more recent years such enthusiasts as Bill Owen, John Pertwee and Tommy Cooper among many others, were regular patrons during their season in Torbay, particularly Tommy who loved the building so much he always gave the staff a pen each.

Another of my early memories in this wonderful cinema was visiting with my gran, who often bought a sixpenny ticket just to watch the Movietone News reels, and I can remember only too well the mid-1930s war in China with all the refugees being shot at along the highway as they tried to escape the war zones. The 1930s also saw the first films with sound. I remember watching such dramas as *The Passing of the Third Floor Back*, *Gone With The Wind* and *Brief Encounter*, weeping along with everyone else as the lovers parted on the station. Following on from this were the epic musical shows in colour, but sadly in 1939 came the Second World War.

By 1944, now in our teens, my school pal and I were allowed to visit the cinema on our own. At this time it was often full of American soldiers all whistling and shouting, with the smell of sweat and Camel cigarettes and usherettes enjoying their attentions. One usherette in particular demanded both spotlights to be on her when she entered the auditorium and, attired with her refreshments tray stacked high, with the grace of a lumbering elephant skipped inelegantly down the aisle giving all the backchat she could to the servicemen, but rest assured she sold all her merchandise! Another year later and I was in this cosy cinema holding the sweaty hand of my very first date.

PINK CHAMPAGNE

During a rehearsal for the drinking scene in act three of *Pink Champagne* at the Palace Theatre, the character Frosch had to flop down on a form. The actor, being a big chap, came down a bit too hard and to the merriment of the audience fell backwards finishing with legs in mid-air, for he appeared decidedly drunk. To the director it was a disaster, and before the next performance came the remark, 'No gold stars for acrobatics on stage tonight, thank you!'

CIDER CAPERS!

Theo made friends with a chap called Sid during the Second World War when they were both stationed at Bulford, Wiltshire, in 1942. They discovered a mutual liking for opera and together went to see *The Beggar's Opera*. They didn't meet again until Theo came to Paignton in 1954 and joined the Paignton Operatic Society, where he again met Sid; the two men again became good friends.

During operatic productions in the Palace Avenue Theatre, it was quite the thing for one or two members of the cast to stock up with liquid refreshment, which they shared throughout the week. At the beginning of the 1958 production one of the cast, Theo's friend Sid, arrived carrying the usual stone jar of scrumpy in a sack over his shoulder (almost certainly from Churchwards in Yalberton), for Sid and his friend Charlie to share during the performances. Come the last night, they had a quantity left over and rather than put good scrumpy down the sink, drank it all before taking their final bow as the Salzgammergut Fire Brigade – but couldn't make it to the stage, let alone put a fire out!

CHAPTER TWENTY-FOUR
Hand–Made

Just before the end of the nineteenth century, in the summer of 1898 or 1899, two young sisters were running a seaside refreshment kiosk on Ilfracombe beach and no doubt attracted the attention of many an eligible young man. It so happened a young London tailor named John Perrett, better known to his friends as Jack, who originated from Melksham in Wiltshire, decided he needed a holiday by the sea and chose Ilfracombe. Possibly over an ice cream or a cup of tea he met and talked with the two girls in their beach kiosk. Very soon he learnt they were Evelyn and Mel Drew, descendants of an old-established Paignton family.

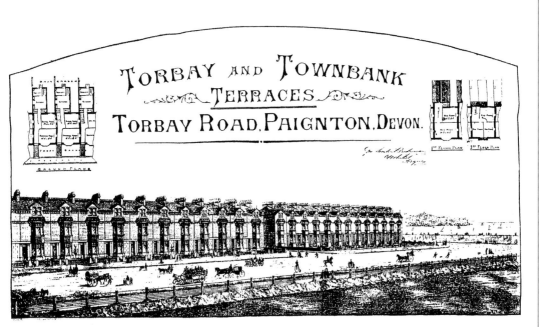

Sales advert for properties in Torbay Road. (*J. Perrett*)

It must have been a case of love at first sight, for later John and Evelyn exchanged photographs from afar; Evelyn's was taken by a photographer in Ilfracombe, while Jack's was in a London studio. Romance ensued and within three years they were married and moved into the lower end of Torbay Road, where they rented a property just a few shops down from where Pelosi's ice-cream parlour eventually opened, next door to Goss Mabin, then a well-known jeweller. Here in 1901 Jack opened a small shop. Having recently completed his apprenticeship with a celebrated London tailor, where one of his jobs was to cut breeches for the Prince of Wales, later King Edward VII, John and Evelyn moved into the flat above the shop. John, being an experienced tailor and cutter, opened the shop as a small fashionable outfitters dealing only in ladies and gentlemen's hand-made clothes, and proudly advertised that his price for making a lady's hand-braided, full-length velour suit was 50s. While here their two children, Dorothy and Wilfred Mornington Perrett, were born. The business quickly expanded and Jack soon realised he needed larger premises. So, shortly after their children's arrival, he decided to move his family and business into a bigger shop along the road where, for most of the time, he had plenty of work making those full length velour suits, a popular style then, worn with buttoned-up black boots.

When Jack took over the second shop much of the area below Station Square was still sand dunes. At first Jack rented this shop, which was opposite Mr Lambshead's recently completed Queen's Park Mansions, so it is very likely these two men could have chatted now and then. At about the same time Lambshead

Torbay Road before Deller's Café was built in about 1912. (*J. Perrett*)

was looking to raise capital for the new state of the art café (Deller's) that he intended to build on a site next to his row of mansions. It is therefore possible this is when he offered Jack the freehold on the rented shop, which previously had been Lambshead's butchery business. Jack bought the premises in about 1905 for the sum of £1,200 and after the contract was signed Lambshead remarked, 'You'd never have acquired this property if I hadn't needed the money to build my café!' And so it was that Jack became the proud owner of 21 Torbay Road, known today as The House of Orange.

In the new workshop handmade suits were measured, cut and fitted by Jack, then stitched together by jacket hands, waistcoat hands and trouser hands; each hand being a fully qualified tailor who could make and complete a suit. Tailors never stood up to do their work, but sat in a crossed-leg position on a huge wooden dais that was raised up off the floor, where they sewed and pressed each section of their work. The pressing was done on a short board on their knees, over which they would place the section of the garment they were working on, covering it with a damp cloth. Originally they pressed the material with goose irons, very heavy flat-irons used by tailors, but gas irons were beginning to replacing them. The continuous use of these strange hissing irons filled the workshop with a constant smell of wet wool.

A goose iron used by tailors in the nineteenth century. (*Peggy Parnell*)

Some of Jack's tailors in the early days, and even in the later years, lived as far away as St Marychurch. One employee in particular, Tommy Kerslake, would walk in and back again every day, summer and winter, rarely missing a day until he was too old to work. He was an endearing character, thought of very highly by Jack and Evelyn and sadly missed when he died. From 1905 onwards knowledge of Jack's fine workmanship quickly spread, and in newly developed Paignton there was a demand for such a high standard of work. Unfortunately customers at this time never considered paying an account for at least six months and in some cases even a year. Consequently Jack and his wife were finding things very hard, and one month the only money they took from the business was a halfpenny for one button! In fact things were so bad they made do with bread and boiled cabbage. Obviously something had to be done, so Evelyn decided to rent an apartment house (a boarding house), 6 Adelphi Terrace; moving the whole family in, she proceeded very successfully to take in guests. Jack continued his tailoring business behind the shop, but let off a section at the front as a cigarettes and sweets kiosk.

Fourteen years or so later, in about 1915, they moved back into the flat over No. 21 and here Wilfred and Dorothy grew up, attended local schools and met their future partners in life. Wilfred attended Paignton College in Hyde Road, now Crossways shopping centre, and made friends with the sons of other well-known businessmen like the Evans boys (well-known Paignton bakers). Like all young lads he got into trouble many a time. One particular escapade involved the Stoke Gabriel bus, which in those days used to come from Station Square down Torbay Road and turn right into Queens Road. As it travelled down Torbay Road the boys would dash out, jump up and cling onto the back of the bus, just as the driver swung around the corner. In order not to hurt themselves should they fall off, Wilfred, known to his friends as Wilf, borrowed cushions from his mother's sitting-room, which they strapped to their bottoms for protection. Needless to say when found out they were not exactly popular! On leaving school Wilf was apprenticed to a large drapery store known as Bobby & Co. (now Debenhams) on the Strand in Torquay.

In the early 1920s Jack decided to branch out, in a small way, into ready-made items of men's wear, but as he was getting older he was determined that Wilf and Dorothy should both be employed in the shop. Dorothy, however, fell in love with a young electrician named Harry Cove Clark, so instead Grandfather Jack, as he became known, as a wedding present, set them up in a business partnership in Hyde Road with Harry's two brothers George, an electrician, and Gerald, a plumber, with Dorothy running the shop for them. Meanwhile Grandfather Jack continued tailoring hand-made quality clothes, while his son Wilf built up a retail men's department.

In 1927 Wilf married a professional pianist called Gladys who worked in London. They purchased a house in Butland Avenue for the princely sum of £850. Two years later Gladys gave birth to their first baby, Peggy. Then on Thursday 25 October 1934 Gladys gave birth to a boy, John, who, she always claimed, was ceremoniously born in Paignton Hospital with parish church bells ringing peals of joy. She probably didn't realise the bell ringers always practised on Thursday evenings! Another year on, in 1935, a brand new shop front was fitted, so up to date that it was featured in the September edition of the *Menswear* magazine.

An old J. Perrett & Son sales ledger, dated between 1935 and 1936 and written in a fine example of copperplate hand as taught in schools at this time (and up until the 1960s), revealed a Montpelier School account for 1936 audited by F.L. Rossiter, probably when he was a bank employee before joining his family business in Palace Avenue as their financial advisor. Also recorded in the same ledger was an account relating to the future captain of the England Rugby team, Richard Sharp, who had the elbow and seat of his regulation school suit repaired at a total cost of 6s 6d.

In the mid-1930s J. Perrett & Son stocked clothes manufactured by S. Simpson Ltd of London and Wilf, as a long-term wholesale customer, was invited to attend the opening of their new store in Piccadilly. By all accounts it was a very grand affair attended by many VIPs of the day. A fabulous meal was served in the store. The menu, long since disappeared, showed that some very remarkable and expensive vintage wines accompanied the food. Shortly after this Simpson's representative, making one of his regular calls, informed Wilf that his company was now intending to market ladies' suits and skirts and that he would have to place the range somewhere else as Wilf's shop did not stock ladies' wear, which meant Simpson's would have to remove the firm's sole agency for Daks trousers. However, the representative did suggest that if Wilf bought ten or eleven pieces of ladies' wear that would suffice to keep his agency. Suddenly the firm was retailing manufactured ladies' wear!

Four years on things began to alter yet again, this time, thanks to Hitler and the outbreak of war. With Wilf being called up, Jack, who was now at retirement age, had to keep an eye on the whole business. Wilf's wife Gladys, under Grandfather Jack's advice, was also roped in to help in the shop and did so for the duration, employing a housekeeper to look after the children. Daughter Peggy, some five years older than John, was boarded out at Maynards School in the centre of Exeter and was there in May 1944 when the city was heavily blitzed. The family were worried sick, as they could see from their home in Preston the red glow in the sky above the Torquay hills. Within days Peggy wrote a long letter to her father detailing her experiences at this time.

One of the family's clearest wartime memories is that of a hit-and-run raid on Torquay, which took place on the afternoon of Sunday 30 May 1943. Young John Perrett was playing on Goodrington sands and remembers seeing Luftwaffe planes streaking across the bay from the direction of Brixham before bombing Torquay and St Mary's Church, which resulted in the loss of many lives.

From the end of 1943 until the night of 5/6 June 1944 the whole of south Devon was taken over as training grounds by the American troops, particularly in and around the Slapton area where they rigorously practised with live ammunition on the sand dunes. Many Americans lost their lives here in the run up to D-Day. But of course youngsters in Paignton, Torquay and Brixham thought having 'Yankees' living in their midst was great, and watched with interest as the soldiers learnt how to handle their strange amphibian cars – flat-bottomed boats on wheels known as DUKWs – on the sands and in the water. But best of all were the goodies handed out by the Americans through schools and various associations in the form of oranges, bananas, cakes and chocolates and in particular strange tins of meat called Spam. Some children even managed to purloin waterproof torches from tanks and trucks. John also recalls the sad deaths of several people brought about by some American troops driving like maniacs around Paignton and the surrounding countryside, including two of his friends from Montpelier School, as well as the night he was walking near the Milk Bottle at the bottom of Cecil Road and saw to his horror a man lying in the road, having been mown down by a speeding Jeep and killed.

Throughout the many difficulties of the war years, the business continued to tick over, even though merchandise became very difficult to obtain, much of it being Government standard with the black eclipsed double-moon 'utility' label, and of course because of the clothing coupons that had to be accounted for. Like everyone else the Perrett family had to endure food rationing, which continued well after the cessation of hostilities. Jack Perrett continued running the business until son Wilf returned from his military service to take over the reins. But 1946 was to see even more changes, for shortly after Wilf returned home both his parents died, within a couple of months of one another.

Wilf now put his heart and soul into expanding the business and in 1949 bought a second property, known as the Happidrome Amusements Arcade, where he established a brand new ladies' wear shop. This department, now on its own, grew rapidly, selling such well-known labels as Daks Burberry and Hebe suits and skirts. Within two years he bought Windsor's butcher shop next door and immediately doubled his floor space. At about the same time (about 1950), Harry and Auntie Doss, as she was affectionately known to her nephews, moved next door into 45 Torbay Road, where they traded as Cove Clark, sports gear, toys and gifts.

When Wilf's son John left school in 1951 he very much wanted to join his father in the business, but Wilf had ideas of a professional qualification for his son and placed him as an articled clerk with his godfather, Charles Drew, a quantity surveyor. John never took to the job. In a way luck was on his side when the firm's offices were destroyed in the Waycotts Corner fire. John leapt at the opportunity to tell his dad that he had finished with quantity surveying and really wanted to work in the shop. Wilf looked very pensively at his young son as he listened to his pleas. John, on the other hand, stood quaking in his shoes. Suddenly Wilf said, 'Right, get on home, boy, and change into your best suit, then report to the tie counter in half an hour'. So in 1952, at the tender age of seventeen, John Perrett entered his family's retail clothing business, only to leave it shortly afterwards to do his National Service in the Royal Artillery; but on completion of his two years' service he took and enjoyed a training period with Simpson's of Piccadilly, after which he quickly returned to his retailing career. However, before leaving for Simpson's in London, he met a young Brixham girl called Valerie. They eventually married in All Saints' Church, Brixham. It was indeed a day to be remembered for it was noticed that as John knelt at the altar, the men's wear retailer from Paignton had a hole in his sock!

In the October just a few months before John's wedding, Wilf went to view the house they were having built in Preston. Unfortunately he fell off a ladder, which brought on a serious heart attack from which he never really recovered, and although John had the strength of his dad's very sound advice in the background, Wilf never returned to full-time business and John found himself, at the age of twenty-two, up the creek without a paddle. The first thing John did was to revamp the men's shop, not without some fear and trepidation as to what his father would say when he saw it!

Sometime in 1962 an article in the *Western Morning News* featured a vacant corner property that was for sale in Teignmouth. The property was viewed and purchased, and Perrett's extended to another town.

At about this time John's younger brother, Peter, qualified as a chartered accountant and was asked if he would like to join the business. Although he had been offered a job elsewhere, he agreed, and so a company was formed with Peter as its financial director. The two boys were to stay together and both honestly agree they never had a serious argument to the day they retired.

Tragically, one Tuesday morning in January 1965 John and his wife Valerie were abruptly awakened by John's aunt Dorothy, telephoning to inform them that flames were leaping from the vicinity of their men's shop up the road. Indeed flames were towering 30–40ft in the air. John and Peter were quickly on site, and fortunately the fire only touched the roof, which meant the shop only suffered from water damage. The fire brigade were marvellous, covering the stock with tarpaulins and saving it from damage, but leaving everything very damp. The stock was duly moved into Deller's Café, which at this time was awaiting demolition. They managed to agree with the insurers to pay salvage for the stock, which meant they could conduct a fire damage sale. Never again would Perrett's sell Moorland sheepskin coats for £5, £8 and £12! Very quickly the men's department was moved into the ground floor of the ladies' store. John and Peter took advantage of the rebuilding to have a new Benbow's shop front installed, which of course is the shop front of the present House of Orange.

Among the many members of Perrett's staff was one who was highly thought of by all the family. This was Sid Wotton who had served Wilf and the firm for forty-two years from the very early days in the 1920s. One morning he didn't arrive for work and John, with the van driver, was dispatched to see why he had not turned up. Sid was a widower living alone, and when John and the driver arrived at his home they discovered him in the hallway where he had collapsed and died from a massive heart attack. To the whole company he was a wonderful man, and he was missed very much by everyone. At about the same time, in the late 1960s, Perrett & Son held very hectic sales with customers queuing non-stop from the early hours to lunchtime, right around the corner past Cove Clarks into Garfield Road.

The firm became involved in many charity events. One in particular was the unusual summer event of 1952 when a friendly football match was held on Paignton green between the Round Table and Rotary clubs, which started with the Rotarians and Roundtablers, all attired in fancy dress, gathering at the top of Palace Avenue and climbing aboard two R.G. Ford & Sons lorries, then proceeding down Victoria Street and Torbay Road, pelting one another with bags of flour and water as a way of advertising the game. This successfully drew people onto Paignton Green where they watched a hilarious match played with a 5ft diameter ball, which succeeded in collecting a tidy sum for charity.

There was never a dull day in Perrett's business and the 1970s proved equally lively, with such incidents as the local authority's strike in 1970, which caused much suffering for everyone when the Clennon Valley Sewage employees suddenly downed tools and walked out, leaving the tanks virtually full! Thanks to the local Rotarians, who for some weeks together with other more qualified volunteers, mounted a twenty-four-hour watch over the pumps in four-hour shifts, a disaster was averted. On the first day of the strike John Perrett was attending the initial briefing on the operation of the pumps, when brother Peter arrived. Calling John outside he explained, as gently as he could, that their dad had died suddenly while sitting with a friend in his boat in Brixham harbour. Apparently Wilf had been chatting when suddenly he took ill. He died within minutes. For Wilf what a wonderful way to go, but it came as a terrible shock to all the family.

Note the gleam in George's eyes as he weighs up the two lovelies posing in the window. (*J. Perrett*)

Perrett's fashion show. (*J. Perrett*)

The 1970s saw a period of new fashions coming in, and like other notable fashion retailers Perrett's began to put on regular fashion shows, usually at Oldway Mansion or the Redcliffe Hotel.

Then there was the day a speedboat jumped its towing hitch and crashed through the window of their Teignmouth shop. A press photo showed that the policeman was quickly to hand.

Earlier in the same decade another disaster occurred, albeit a small one: this time it was the collapse of the canopy over the pavement outside the men's shop in Torbay Road. Fortunately it was Wednesday half-day closing, so few people were about, but it was never discovered if one of the supporting pillars was knocked by a parking car or was just a victim of old age.

Over the years Perrett's received all kinds of letters which found their way into John Perrett's curio file. One was a letter from a well-known local character named Bert Lidstone, who wrote:

> Dear Perrett Bros,
> You may be interested in this label, which was on the hat box of an opera hat I bought for stage wear in 1937!
> Yours, Bert

Another revealed the changes over time:

> Sir . . . now, an idea as to the change in the value of the £1. I am not sure of the date involved, but it must have referred to the very early 1950s. I showed one of your staff my original wedding day photograph wearing the dress I bought from you in Torbay Road twenty-five years ago, complete with veil, flowers, undies and stockings, and the total cost was just £10!

One very nice letter was from MSV *Stena Seaspread* in San Carlos Water, East Falkland, dated 14 July 1982, which read, 'I return herewith label attached to a consignment of beer and minerals duly received on board, with our grateful thanks to your good selves and the people of Torbay.'

In 1979/80 the company purchased Eric Thomas' men's wear business at 33 Fore Street, Brixham, together with the leasehold on the House of Orange down on the quay. But within a few years, in 1984, the freehold of 33 Fore Street was sold to Oliver's Shoes. The House of Orange continued to trade on the Quay and was closely followed by a second store being opened in Paignton. Very soon the lease on the quay was disposed of and Jim Sharp, the manager, transferred to the Paignton branch. Shortly afterwards he and his wife took a lease out on the property from the company, and they now run the store as their own business.

In the late 1980s, when Jan and Arthur Rowe, joint managers of the Teignmouth branch, retired, the business was closed down and the property, together with the flat above, was rented out and shortly afterwards sold. John's son David, now in his late twenties, had by this time joined the company and was responsible for buying both men's and ladies' garments. But sadly Jack's fine clothing business was coming to an end, for in 1997 John and Peter retired, the business was closed and the property rented out. David eventually bought a franchise and now runs a business of his own.

CHAPTER TWENTY-FIVE
Trades & Traders

TAIL END!

A Paignton grocery proprietor witnessed the tail of a huge rat disappearing behind a large mirror in his shop window so got his assistant to set a rat trap and place it behind the mirror. At the busiest time of the day, with a shop full of customers, came an almighty bang. Everyone looked around in astonishment, but the proprietor and assistant just stared at one another knowingly. 'Don't explain to the customers!' was written across their faces, but they were thankful they had caught the rat. Later, when the shop was empty, they retrieved the trap from behind the mirror, only to discover the big rat was a tiny mouse!

OVER RIPE!

One particular grocer used to stock Camembert cheeses, which he detested because of the smell and always placed as far away from himself as possible. However, while stocktaking one day he discovered he was down to the last one. Having just collected a list of his customers' weekly orders for delivery the next day, he noted that the housekeeper to one of his best clients, a lover of this particular cheese, had requested a box. 'Whoops', he gasped, taking up the last cheese, 'It's rather riper than it should be!'. In fact it was crawling with maggots! Shaking them out, he proceeded to fill the small holes with salt. On delivering the groceries he explained to his customer's housekeeper, 'if Mr "I" doesn't like the cheese I shan't charge him, but if he does than I'll make a charge.' The following week when collecting his account he enquired, 'By the way, how was the cheese?'.

'Oh,' replied the housekeeper, ''T'were best e'd ever 'ad.'

GRANDMA'S STRAP

Well into the 1950s, some older tradesmen were still using horses and carts for deliveries, like the old greengrocer who called weekly to outlandish places such as Foxhole, laden with all manner of fruit and vegetables. One particular day the old boy asked a young housewife, as she paid for her purchases, had she by any chance a piece of old rope because his 'orse had a broken strap. The young lady replied, 'I can do better than that,' and promptly produced her grandmother's hefty leather case strap. He was delighted – but half an hour later she happened to look out of her window to see the horse galloping in one direction and the greengrocer's cart turned over in a neighbour's garden, spilling fruit and vegetables in all directions. In the middle of the road stood an irate greengrocer waving a bloodied hand and shouting, 'that there' b'dy strap of 'urs b'aint no good, t'were' b'dy well rotten!'

CHAPTER TWENTY-SIX

All Our Yesteryears

THE MEDLAR TREE

Michael Adams, at the time of writing, was in his ninety-second year and one of the few locals who could remember what Paignton was like during the early twentieth century. Although born in Fore Street, St Marychurch in Torquay, from the age of four he spent the rest of his life in Paignton.

In the late 1980s Michael wrote his first novel, a love story called *The Medlar Tree*, a story reflecting the Paignton he knew and loved as a boy.

It was a lovely June afternoon when the author listened to Michael, a tall gentle gentleman with pale blue eyes that twinkled as he recalled his past. He was to have recorded even more interesting memories, but sadly we shall never know what they might have been, for only weeks after this interview he departed this

Deller's original ballroom under the dome. (*T. Moss*)

Deller's fine Art Deco stairway. (*Herald & Express*)

life. Considering the wealth of memories he had, it's not impossible to imagine that one of his stories could well have been about his youth, dancing in Deller's original small, wood-panelled, parquet-floored ballroom, with a fine twenty-one piece orchestra taking up most of the floor, and walking down the fine oak staircase leading to the restaurant below where dancers partook of much-needed refreshments after dancing in the cramped ballroom above; and here no doubt, in the wood-panelled alcoves, many young lovers kissed and cuddled. This is how he describes a certain event in his delightful book *The Medlar Tree*, a book into which he wove so many of his boyhood memories.

IN LIVING MEMORY

Suddenly Anno Domini grips you by the arm, reminding you that your salad days are over and memories come flitting back of the Big Tree and the first generation of horse chestnuts, GWR's goods yard and the old turntable (now Great Western Close), Tanners Lane where you waited with bucket and spade for the railway gates to open, the allotments opposite ablaze with red poppies, and my teens when I cycled to Three Beaches and my aunt's shop, past the Clennon Valley tip with its thousands of seagulls, the marshland and the reed-riddled pond where

The Big Tree before its demise and the loss of the three houses behind. (*Peggy Parnell*)

the waterfowl played hide-and-seek and our dog nearly drowned. Each spring where the myriad of wild flowers burst into life among the piles of rubble (long since gone) and the pheasants our spaniel routed out there. The tangled walk through a jungle of trees and briar that led past the kilns to Herbert Whitley's old zoo entrance, and the faded board which read 'Entrance Fee 6*d*'. Although the new generation of chestnut trees along the Dartmouth Road are now mature, they still bring back memories of all our yesteryears that many of us can recall.

GREEN HILLS AND BLUE SEA

That I should ever be thought of as a local character is about as far-fetched as could be. But West Country I truly am. Destiny determined that I should be born in Bristol on a July day in 1927 and arrived in Paignton a mere few months later. It is in Torquay and Paignton in particular that I first came to know the world around me. With time, thanks to my grandmother, I discovered the green hills and the lovely blue sea, the delights of Cockington, Occombe and Westerland Valleys and later with my friends the many country lanes that always seemed to be full of wild flowers. Paignton is where I went to school, and later where I became a student at the Paignton's School of Art and Science and where, not wishing to decide politically between 'Red Russia' or 'Yellow China', I decided to leave. Another three-year course was found for me, this time at the Torquay Commercial College in Torre, a grand Georgian building with its beautiful eighteenth-century blue and white toilet pan complete with mahogany seat and hole straight into the ground!

Unfortunately money ran out just as I was about to take my diploma. I suggested perhaps I could take a summer job, but was quickly told 'well-brought-up young ladies do not take summer jobs'; sadly a criterion of my grandmother's day. So into the typing pool of a local firm of quantity surveyors I went with the princely wage of £1.50 per week. Ah, well, that was the way of life sixty years ago.

Bibliography

Betty Adams, *History & The Personal Reminiscences of the Catholic Church in Paignton*, 1995

Michael Adams, *Memoirs*, 2002

Jack Baker, *Chimps, Chumps & Elephants*, 1998

Ernest Britton, *The Oldenburg Hotel*, 1990

W.G. Couldrey, *Memories*, 1932

Bill Coysh, Arthur Day's article – *Herald & Express*, 1959

Dymond & White, *Torquay & Neighbours*, 1800

Charles Gregory, 'Brixham in Devonia', 1919

Eric Hemery, *Historic Dart*, 1982

Herald & Express, Bygones 1987–2000

H.D. Higgs, 'Paignton & its Surroundings *c*. 1890–1900'

D.R. Johnson, *William of Orange's Expedition to England 1688*, 1988

Revd C. Arthur Lane, *English Church History*, 2004

C.R. Lewis, *Our Village*, 2000

Revd Mr Lyde-Hunt, Journal *c*. 1920s

N. Orme, *Unity & Varity*, 1991

Joyce Packe, 'The Prince it is That's Coming', *Paignton 1854*, 1988

Paignton Observer

Peggy Parnell, *The Grand Old Lady*, 1986

Peggy Parnell, 'At the Side of the Stage', (Personal Archives)

Charles Patterson, *The History of Paignton*, 1952

John Pentney, *Robinson's Directory of Paignton*, 1992

Frank R. Penwill, *Paignton in Six Reigns*, 1953

John R. Pike, *Portrait of Torbay*, 1975

PP&LHS, *Pembroke Survey 1566*, 2007

Deryck Seymour, *Torre Abbey*, 1977

The Bishop's Palace, Paignton – An Archaeological Report, English Heritage, July 2001

Jean Tregaskes, The Churston Story

Peter Tully, *Pictures of Paignton Part II*, 1988

Wardlock & Co., 'Paignton & South Devon'

Derek Wilson, *The Tower of London*, 1978